THE FRIENDLY
BANKER

THE FRIENDLY BANKER

Richard Baughman

INSOMNIAC PRESS

Edited by Mike O'Connor.
Copy edited by Rudy Mezzetta.
Designed by Mike O'Connor.

Canadian Cataloguing in Publication Data

Baughman, Richard, 1951-
  The friendly banker

Includes index.
ISBN 1-895837-47-2

1. Finance, Personal. 2. Debt. 3. Mortgage loans. I. Title.

HG179.B385 1999   332.024'02   C99-931679-6

The publisher gratefully acknowledges the support of the Canada Council and the Ontario Arts Council.

Printed and bound in Canada

The Canada Council | Le Conseil des Arts
FOR THE ARTS | DU CANADA
SINCE 1957 | DEPUIS 1957

ONTARIO ARTS
COUNCIL
CONSEIL DES ARTS
DE L'ONTARIO

Insomniac Press, 393 Shaw Street,
Toronto, Ontario, Canada, M6J 2X4
www.insomniacpress.com

Table of Contents

Acknowledgements

The writing of a book is a fascinating intellectual odyssey. Yet, the author alone is seldom solely responsible for the ideas that come together to form the words that fill the pages from cover to cover. For we are all influenced by the people we come in contact with throughout our lives.

I want to first thank my wife and soulmate, Dale and my precious daughter, Cheylene for their patience, understanding, love and support throughout this project.

Thanks also to my copy editor, Rudy Menzetta, for helping shape and mould the manuscript into a finished product.

As well, I wish to thank all the wonderful men and women I worked with over twenty five years in the financial services industry. Your influence will never be forgotten.

To my friends, family, Joyce and Christie and my colleagues who have been encouraging me to write professionally for years, despite my stubborn ongoing refusals, my most profound gratitude to all of you.

To business philosopher and lecturer Jim Rohn. I am forever grateful for your guidance and influence over these last several years. You helped me find the words and the way.

A special thanks to author, lecturer and personal development specialist, Brian Tracy, for his generosity in allowing his theory of 'The E Factor' to be incorporated into this book. Brian's guidance, influence and support were instrumental in the writing process and his teachings have helped enhance the quality of my life for many years. I am forever and profoundly grateful.

Finally, I wish to thank my editor and publisher, Mike O'Connor. You took a chance on a first time author with a dream and made the delivery of a very important message possible for all those who would invest the time to read it. Your contribution has been large, indeed.

To Kenneth and Edna Baughman in loving memory.

Introduction

"The worst days of those who enjoy what they do are better than the best days of those who don't." — Jim Rohn

"Mr. Whitby, please."

"Yes, may I say who wants to see him?"

"Richard Baughman."

"Do you have an appointment?"

"Yes, for 11 a.m."

"Fine, Mr. Baughman. Please have a seat and Mr. Whitby will be with you in a moment."

Mr. Whitby was my banker. I was just a very young man of twenty-one, a tire salesman on vacation on a hot summer day in July, 1972, when I came in to ask him for some advice. You see, it used to be very common for people to visit their bankers when they wanted guidance on almost any subject. We were taught that bankers were wise. How else could they manage our money? They were respected members of the community and everybody, at least most people I knew, looked up to them. There was just an element of trust associated with a bank manager that was never really questioned.

On this day, I was faced with a problem. I had an important decision to make and I thought it best to summon up the courage to see Mr. Whitby because he could probably set me on the right course. I remained in the waiting area for only a few minutes, but it seemed like a few hours. I could see Mr. Whitby through the window of his office talking with a client.

This was an important, perhaps life-changing day, for me and I devoted some of the time in the waiting room thinking about the progress I had made in my life. I had graduated high school and, labouring under the delusion that I had learned enough to make my way, had given up a chance to go to university in favour of starting a job, first assembling cars, and now selling tires. But even at twenty-one, I was already thinking, "Where will this all lead? Probably not very far, to be sure. Will it always be this way? Bouncing from job to job with no clear direction? Perhaps on this day I'll find some answers." I needed to find the answers.

"Mr. Baughman, Mr. Whitby will see you now."

I snapped back out of my reflective mode, and followed the receptionist into Mr. Whitby's office like a man being led to his own execution. To say I was nervous would be an understatement. It was very normal to be nervous while seeing your banker over banking issues, let alone asking for his time and wisdom about a life problem. How would he respond?

I entered the office, the secretary introduced us and we shook hands. He was a giant! As I think back, he couldn't have been more than six-foot-three but at the time he seemed ten feet tall to me. I looked up into his eyes and sheepishly announced my name as he greeted me with a firm handshake.

"Have a seat, young man. What can I do for you today?"

I could see already he was very stern and to the point. With sweat pouring down my brow, my neck and seemingly down into my shoes, I said "I need some advice about a job offer, sir."

"A job offer? Very good. What kind of job is it?"

"Well, sir, it's for assistant manager at Friendly Finance."

"Friendly Finance? Really? Very interesting! Tell me first how you came to receive this job offer and then we'll discuss the offer itself, okay?"

He leaned back into his high-backed leather chair and settled in to hear my story. It looked as if he was now accepting the fact I was in his office, and that he was going to be devoting some time to help me. I began to settle down, and as I did, it became easier to talk to him.

"Well, I'm on vacation right now and when I walked in to Friendly Finance the other day to make my payment..."

"Wait a minute," he said. "You have a loan there?"

"Yes sir, for a car." For a moment, I was convinced I that I had already gotten myself into trouble. I was embarrassed to admit that I had taken out a loan from a finance company. After all, the interest rate was really high, about 24 percent. I really thought I was going to receive a tongue lashing from Mr. Whitby about this.

"Go on."

I breathed a sigh of relief.

"Well, sir, as I was standing at the front counter at Friendly Finance, making my loan payment and just chatting with the receptionist, I mentioned to her that I had seen an ad they were running in the newspaper for an assistant manager. Just as I said that the manager got up from his desk and walked over to the counter. I think he was looking at my loan records or something."

"What did he say?"

"He didn't say anything for a few minutes. He picked up my records and looked at them, then looked at me and then at my records again. I thought I had done something wrong. Then he invited me to sit down and said, 'You may just be the man we're looking for.'

Mr. Whitby smiled. I wondered what he was thinking.

"He interviewed you right there?"

"Yes. We talked for about half-an-hour and then he offered me the job. He wanted me to start right then and there! What do you think, Mr. Whitby?"

"Before I tell you, give me some background. What have you been doing since you graduated high school?"

I recounted the brief and rather unexciting details of my young and seemingly directionless life, just as I had replayed them in my own mind while sitting in the waiting room. Mr. Whitby sat motionless in his chair, eyes fixed on me and ears tuned in to every word. When I finished, he sat upright, adjusted his seating position and leaned forward.

"I am very familiar with Friendly Finance. It's a good company and the manager, Mr. Beachwood, is an excellent manager. I know him very well."

I was stunned to hear this news from Mr. Whitby. Work for a finance company? The very last thing I expected to hear that was what sounded like a ringing endorsement.

"I thought you would not be pleased to hear that I was considering a job offer from a finance company. What can you tell me about them?"

"Friendly Finance has been in business, I think, for about fifty years. They have branches all over the world. The training is excellent; a very good way to start your financial career, if that is what you want. Is it what you want?"

"To be honest, sir, I don't know. I've never really known what it is I want to do. But it sounds like a good idea to me. I'm willing to give it a try, and see if I like the work. That's about the best I can say."

"Why did you think I would be angry that you were considering a job offer from a finance company?"

"Well, sir, I've done some checking around and people tell me that they charge high interest rates. I've even heard the term 'loan sharks' used. I thought you would say the same."

Mr. Whitby leaned back into his chair, into a very relaxed position and said, "Young man, you have been obviously talking to the wrong people. There's nothing wrong with working for a finance company and there is certainly nothing wrong with the service they provide for the community."

I was blown away by what he told me. This was coming from a banker! Then he said something I will never forget.

"Would it surprise you to know that banks forced finance companies into existence?"

"Excuse me, sir? How did they do that?" For a moment I thought he was joking!

"Around the turn of the century, banks were only for the rich. They were not really interested in lending money to the average working family. In fact, if you wanted a loan, you had to have enough in your bank account to cover it because the bank wanted your savings as security." I would later find out that that practice remained with us far into this century.

"But sir, if you had the money in your bank account, why would you need the loan?"

"Precisely, Richard. As a result not many people qualified for loans. The system was set up to deny them."

"So, what did they do?"

"There was a kind of revolution against the banking system. People decided they were not going to take that kind of treatment from the banks, and so consumer groups were formed. They pooled their resources and formed the first finance companies. As groups, they were able to put up enough security to borrow from the banks, enough to get started. Then they made small loans to ordinary people. Thus, the problem of access to loans was solved."

"But what about the cost? Were the rates high then?"

"Of course, Richard. They had to be. After all, they borrowed the money from the banks at high rates to begin with. Let me give you an example. If you borrow money at 12 percent per annum, you cannot charge 12 percent to lend it out. There's no margin for profit. So, you have to charge more."

"But double? Twenty-four percent?"

"Please remember, Richard. These were small loans. The percentages may sound high but in actual dollars the margins were very fine indeed. They had to charge 24 percent to stay in business, to pay their expenses and their employees."

"So, banks forced finance companies into existence?"

"They certainly did. And over the years they have grown into very large companies, serving the needs of millions of people."

"Mr. Whitby, what about today? Doesn't the bank lend to ordinary people?"

"They do to some extent Richard, and they are trying to improve, but it's a slow process. Finance companies are still very active. I think there will always be a need for their services. Now, let's talk about your offer."

"They are willing to pay $450 per month to start, with a review in six months."

"That's not a bad offer. I recommend you give it serious consideration. I can't say much more beyond what we've already discussed. In the final analysis, it's your decision, but if you decide to take it, you have my full support. Maybe some day when you have received the benefit of training and guidance from Mr. Beachwood, you can come and work for the bank."

"Thank you, sir. That would be great. Thank you once again for your time and your advice. I really appreciate everything you've done for me."

"You're welcome, Richard. Good luck!"

With those final words from Mr. Whitby, I left his office that day and began an incredible odyssey that would span a career of twenty-five years in the financial services industry. Mr. Whitby taught me my very first lesson in banking. That lesson would repeat itself over and over again throughout my career. My friends were wrong about finance companies. I had been wrong in my expectations of Mr. Whitby. I certainly would never have guessed that it was the refusal of banks to lend to ordinary people that caused the formation of finance companies in the first place, that finance companies were in fact performing a very necessary service for the community in helping people establish a credit record.

I would never have guessed that the career on which I was about to embark would take me places I never dreamed of, allow me to enjoy life experiences I could never have imagined and teach me lessons I could not have learned in any university or in any book.

I would never have guessed that in the next twenty-five years I would live in seven different cities and work for seven different companies, from finance companies to banks to credit unions to trust companies. I would never have guessed that I would have the opportunity to work with and learn from some of the finest people in the industry. It *was* indeed a wonderful journey.

I want to share with you some of what I have learned. Will you invest the time? Mr. Whitby and I would like that.

The day I decided to leave banking in 1997, I promised myself two things. First, I would not allow the lessons I had learned and the expertise I had gathered over twenty-five years go to waste. Second, I would share as much information as I could with Canadians, information that would hopefully have a positive impact on their financial future. This would be my way of giving something back to the people who really paid my salary, in appreciation for twenty-five truly fantastic years.

In order to accomplish my goals, I decided on two missions. The first was to open my own business and help people fulfil their dreams of becoming homeowners. I do that to this day by arranging mortgage financing for my clients. Mortgage lending was my favourite activity in banking. It always gave me a wonderful feeling to know I had played a role in helping someone purchase a home and take a major step along the road to financial independence. You will not be surprised, therefore, to learn that mortgages and the role they play in your overall financial plan are a key element of what you are about to learn.

My second mission was to write, so I could share my knowledge with everyone who was willing to invest the time to learn.

I wanted to write this book for many years, but I could not while still an employee of a financial institution. The information is too controversial. You will, if you keep an open mind, learn things that can significantly increase your fortunes, if you choose to employ them. These are strategies and principles, many of which the financial establishment would rather you did not know about, that can help you accumulate savings of hundreds of thousands of dollars over a lifetime. It can mean the difference between a retirement in poverty and a retirement in style. I believe I can safely say that much of what you are about to read has never before been offered to the public. And that is tragic.

To illustrate key points, this book contains case studies and anecdotes. In all cases, the names have been changed to protect confidentiality. It is my hope that you will find this material entertaining and enlightening.

Are you ready? Are you interested? Be forewarned—your own philosophy will determine your degree of acceptance of this material. So keep your mind as open as possible, and by the time you've finished, the big picture may well appear before you!

-1-
A Discovery

"If you wish to find, you must search. Rarely does a good idea interrupt you."
— *Jim Rohn*

During my later years in banking, I began to read books, as I had never read them before. There is something about turning forty that just inspires one to learn all of the things one should have learned twenty years prior.

One day I was watching a video of a seminar prepared by one of the authors that I had been reading, Brian Tracy. Tracy, an author and lecturer on personal development, told of a principle known as the 80/20 rule or the Pareto Principle named after an Italian sociologist and economist. According to Tracy, the 80/20 rule applied to the financial success of the general population in the following manner:

Only about 5 percent of the people in each generation really make it in life. Of 100 people working today, only one will be wealthy when they retire, four will be financially independent, 15 percent will have some savings and 80 percent will be broke and dependent on charities and pensions.

Now, I don't know about you but I found this to be a startling and very depressing statistic. This was not based on a lifetime fraught with one financial tragedy after another. What I was hearing was that the bottom 80 percent of the population wound up broke after a lifetime of productive work. It has never been a secret that most people live from paycheque to paycheque, and certainly I saw enough evidence of that in my banking career. However, the cumulative effects never really dawned on me in the way they were being presented here.

I took this information and began to correlate it with the behaviour patterns of my clients over the years. Having processed more than fifty thousand credit transactions of every kind, from small loans to credit cards to mortgages, I had seen a mountain of statistics that helped me to conclude that the 80/20 rule did, in fact hold. I could easily see that the majority were not going to make it financially and, moreover, I began to discover things they were doing, mistakes they were making that were guaranteed to bring about this rather undesirable result. During the couse of my studies I documented some of the habit patterns of financially successful people as well as those of the "financially challenged."

Let me give you a few examples, beginning with a habit pattern of the successful group. I used to work in a small community composed mostly of retirees, but with a growing influx of younger families as well. The common denominator they shared was that they were quite well off and very educated. Every once in a while someone would need a mortgage, either to buy a new house, or transfer from another institution, or to purchase a revenue property. Mortgages were not very common in this community where fully 60 percent of all real-estate transactions were completed in cash.

I was astonished, on more than one occasion, at how much these people knew about mortgages compared to people I had served in other communities. Even after twenty years in the business, I could barely teach them anything, and in some cases they were teaching me! They knew exactly what they wanted and how to get it. Few if any were ready to settle for a 25-year amortization (the length of time it takes to pay the balance in full), opting to reduce borrowing costs as much as possible. It became apparent to me that these people had all developed the habit of self-education. They brought along with them books they had read to show me they were prepared, and to challenge anything that was at variance with what they had learned. These people knew that a mortgage was one of the largest financial agreements they would ever sign in their lives, and they were not going to make a mistake with it.

Another quality they often had was that they were what we in the financial-services industry call "grinders." After setting a shorter amortization, they would dicker on the rate to the point of exhaustion and would often present research they had done on what was happening in the mortgage market. About the only thing they didn't have was our bottom line and I was guarding that with my life. After all, I was paid to maximize profit, not to give the farm away. After they had finished on the rate issue, they would start in on the fees and argue endlessly to win a concession for a free appraisal, which otherwise cost $150, a concession the bank hated to give.

I can recall coming out of my office on several occasions very frustrated after a gruelling session with one of these clients. After a time, I finally realized the painfully obvious. The habit patterns of these people—the self-education, the grinding right down to the seemingly most insignificant point — all of it was part of the reason that they were financially successful in the first place.

The behaviour patterns of the financially challenged were remarkably different. To these applicants, I would try to explain some of the long-term benefits of our mortgages, of which there were many. As part-and-parcel of my services, I would show people how to pay their mortgages off years sooner than the 25-year standard amortization period. I wanted to provide some financial counselling to add value for our customers and to show them how we were different from our competition. I would show my clients how even a small amount paid additionally on the mortgage every month, even $50, could really pay big dividends in the form of reduced interest charges.

Well, I must tell you that in many cases I was not very successful. In fact, most of these clients opted to just go with the 25 years and the lowest monthly payment possible. Further, most never even flinched when I mentioned the $150 appraisal fee. They paid it without argument.

This same group, I found, could also be easily swayed by some of the mortgage gimmickry that was being advertised in the marketplace. For example, a lender would say to them, "I'll give you a 1/4 percentage point off and show you how to save $10,000 over the life of your mortgage *or* I will subsidize your legal fees up to $300." This group would almost invariably grab the $300 and run! They would actually waive an opportunity to shorten their mortgage by two or three years so that they could have a comparatively small amount of money today.

Those in the bottom 80-percent group could be roped in very easily by unscrupulous lenders offering a tiny carrot and miss the big picture entirely, even paying higher-than-market rates in some cases. All too often, this behaviour would result in years of unnecessary mortgage payments for them, a very sad result indeed.

Would you say that the bottom 80-percent were ignorant? Would you say misinformed? Could it be they had a live-for-today philosophy? One would have to wonder why they would sit there with eyes glazed over and waive a very substantial long-term benefit in favour of a comparatively small short-term benefit. For many years I had seen this tendency towards short-term thinking, to the exclusion of any consideration of the long-term consequences, in most of my borrowing clients, but I had never really thought about why it was. I only knew that if you could fit a monthly payment into the budget of people in this group, you could sell them almost anything, at any price.

And the market did. They still do today. In the course of my studies reading dozens of books outside of my banking activities I came across an explanation that made sense. It was written, again, by Brian Tracy, a favourite author of mine. It's called "The E Factor."

"The E Factor"

The "E" in "E Factor" is short for expediency. Tracy explained that through his years of research, he had found that the bottom 80 percent group is afflicted somehow with a tendency to always try to get what they want the fastest and easiest way. They are consumed with a desire for instant gratification, to the exclusion of any consideration of the long-term consequences. This tendency often results in short-term gain and long-term pain. I came to the conclusion that in financial terms, this tendency towards expedience could translate into a propensity to overuse credit cards, to be unable to resist the temptation to haul out the plastic every time they saw something they wanted. In my judgement it could also explain why someone would waive a $10,000 long-term benefit in exchange for $300 today.

Now, we don't know why it is that the numbers work the way they do. We don't know why it is that a tiny percentage of the population would seize the $10,000 opportunity and the rest would give it all up for $300. All we know is that's the way it is! We also know that the group most susceptible to "The E Factor" will wind up broke and in debt after a lifetime of these bad financial habits. I have seen it more times than I care to recall, but fear not, I am going to try to help you avoid it.

The retail industry takes major advantage of "The E Factor." Just pick up your local newspaper on any given day and look at the ads. What do you see? Many of them are advertising some sort of short-term benefit or inducement to purchase their product or service right now. They often claim to have limited supplies, and represent that the offers are good only for a short period of time, probably never to be repeated. Many of them use credit as the facilitator to a purchase transaction by offering low monthly payments or no payments at all for extended periods of time. People in the bottom 80 percent group tend not to realize that such inducements are of very little actual value and that in most cases the cost of these programs is built into the price of the goods they are purchasing anyway.

Before I continue, I want to make sure you understand my intentions. I do not seek to denigrate certain groups, only to point out how the habit patterns of certain people can have long-term consequences, good or bad. When I mention "the bottom 80 percent," I refer only to financial standing in relation to the overall population. It makes sense that not everyone in the bottom 80 percent category, financially speaking, has the same degree of susceptibility to "The E Factor." Certainly everyone has it and will be affected by it in varying degrees.

Saving

There is an abundance of money-management books in the marketplace today — virtually every wealth creation scheme you can think of, written by some very well-meaning and talented authors. These books all have a central theme: pay yourself first. It's a sound principle and it does work. Even small amounts invested over a long period of time, re-invested through the wonders of compound interest, will certainly turn into a sizable fortune. There can be no argument — the numbers do not lie. Invest 10 percent of your income over twenty years and just watch what happens!

However, there is something very fundamental that's missing from this plan. Even if you are gainfully employed—certainly not guaranteed in these times — and do manage to sock away the 10 percent, you may find your efforts to live off the remaining 90 percent may not be successful. Many of my clients have told me they have diligently tried to save this amount without success. Why? *Because of their debts.*

It doesn't make very much sense to save 10 percent of your income and then spend your time fending off angry creditors who are missing the money you allocated to savings. They will be on you quickly! So what has to happen before we can implement the wonderful advice of our wealth-creation experts? We must rid ourselves of debt.

This is the key point that I find missing from the advice given by the wealth-creation experts. They do not seem to focus enough on debt, the one thing that prevents 80 percent of the population from saving. In the presence of debt, saving is very unlikely.

In addition, because of the nature of work today, people may change occupations many times during their working lives. Along with this unsettled employment condition are gaps in the income stream that may erode or completely eliminate accumulated savings. So, we need a better plan. That's why I suggest the very foundation of any wealth-creation strategy should be debt management.

I am convinced that the absence of knowledge about debt management is the single largest contributing factor to the failure of the bottom 80 percent group. In my career, I have watched people enslave themselves to a lifetime of interest payments amounting to hundreds of thousands of dollars, unnecessarily. I have seen mistakes made with all forms of consumer credit including loans, credit cards and mortgages. These are mistakes that tend to fill the coffers of the financial institutions to overflowing, while the borrowers relegate themselves, interest payment by interest payment, to a life of poverty and despair in retirement.

The good news is that this does not have to be the case for you. In reality, there are only about a half-dozen things that need to be changed to alter this bleak retirement scenario from one of poverty and despair to one of plenty, peace of mind and happiness.

You may have previously thought that there is a quantum difference between someone living from paycheque-to-paycheque and someone who has a sizable net worth, is financially independent and prepared for most any contingency. I'm here to tell you that this is not the case and that a lifetime virtually free of financial worries can be had by most anyone who can maintain a fairly consistent income, if they change certain habits. Part of the answer is to find a way to substantially reduce the amount you pay on loans, mortgages and credit cards over a lifetime and then convert that savings to investments that yield a decent return. Rest assured we are going to focus on debt by discussing

- **How to prevent debt.**
- **How to manage it.**
- **How to get rid of it.**
- **How to save thousands, tens, even hundreds of thousands of dollars in unnecessary interest charges over a lifetime and make it all wind up in your bank account, complete with compounded interest.**

Interested? Please read on! I am about to show you innovative ways to pay less to the banks and keep more for yourself.

-2-

Your Home Mortgage

"The philosophy of the rich versus the poor is this: the rich invest their money and spend what's left; the poor spend their money and invest what's left." – Jim Rohn.

I once read that a properly structured mortgage is the centrepiece of any personal wealth- creation strategy. What a glorious piece of advice that is. I could not agree more. For most people, the home, and the financing laid in place to go with it, is the centrepiece of your financial well-being.

When we talk about some of these principles of wealth creation, we must acknowledge that not everyone who employs them will become wealthy. They will, in fact, enjoy varying degrees of success. However, the major point here is that, especially for those in the 80 percent group, many of whom may have trouble saving, paying off a home is a means of enforced savings. There is no choice but to do it. Every payment you make adds to your net worth. Thus, your home is an investment in your future.

I believe most people who are realistic in setting their goals would strive towards some very simple ones to begin with. For example, if you could get to a place where all debts are paid off, including your mortgage, and where you would have enough to operate with every month plus a little left over, that would be a very desirable goal, would it not? Anything you could save after that would be gravy, and it would be a lot easier to save in the absence of debt. We aren't talking necessarily about fantastic wealth here, but a level of comfort that brings peace of mind. Since peace of mind is probably the highest good that you have, this is something well worth striving for. Nevertheless, even this level of financial success escapes far too many people.

This is because people make too many mistakes with, primarily their mortgage, but also with consumer debt. These mistakes accumulate over time and tend to short circuit the saving process. The debt remains in place, stubbornly, until a problem arises with income—say upon retirement or job loss—and the standard of living erodes.

This condition, like many diseases, is preventable. There are things you can do, things you are about to learn, that will help you evade the ugly debt monster and fashion a comfortable lifestyle for yourself and your family, a lifestyle that may have been beyond your imagination.

Some of these things may seem small at first glance. That's part of the secret to success. Some of the smallest things are huge in their accumulated effect. Even $30 a month, as you will discover, can make a difference you will not believe! Most people cannot account for $30 a week in walking-around money that has mysteriously left their pockets. Grab it, put it to work in the right places, and doors will open you never thought possible.

Isn't this good news? Isn't it uplifting to learn that there are things the average person can do with just a little discipline that will make a measurable difference in their lives? A comfortable lifestyle is not just for the well-heeled in that top 20 percent group. Most anybody can do it.

But first, to get your attention, I want to demonstrate how the minor pain of discipline is nothing compared to the agony of regret. Here's Joan's story:

The Story of Joan

I was in my office one day working away and lost in it all, when the receptionist entered to announce that there was a client to see me who did not have an appointment. That didn't bother me since I frequently accommodated people in this fashion — we were *supposed* to be in the service business, after all.

In walked Joan, who was in a hurry that day. She apparently had a major list of "things to do." One of her "things to do" was to renew her mortgage. So with a mortgage renewal statement in hand, and without sitting down, Joan announced: "I don't have much time, my car is double parked. I just want to renew my mortgage."

"Fine," I said. I could already see that Joan was not willing to spend any time talking about her mortgage renewal. In fact, I found it hard to believe what I was witnessing.

Joan signed her renewal form, checked the five-year term out of the list of "choices," threw a cheque for $85 on my desk for the renewal fee, and said, "Is that it? I've got to run"

I said, "Yes, that's all you need to do. Thank you for coming in today."

With that, Joan was gone, off to her next stop.

Can you guess how many mistakes Joan made here? Here are some points for your consideration:

- **Joan placed no more importance on her mortgage renewal that day than she did on visiting the dry cleaners.**
- **She failed to devote enough time to make an appointment so we could sit down and properly discuss her mortgage renewal.**
- **Joan selected the posted rate on the renewal form at a time when it would not have taken much effort at all to talk me into a rate discount of 1/2 percent or more. In fact, we were running a promotion at that time and, had Joan only opened a package account with us to do her everyday banking business, I could have authorized a discount of 3/4 of 1 percent off!**
- **Joan also missed an opportunity to apply that 3/4 of 1 percent savings to reduce her amortization, a feature I would have gladly shown her if she only had the time. The effect would have been to reduce her mortgage amortization by about three years at a savings of, oh, $21,000.**
- **Joan freely presented a cheque for the renewal fee, which I would have happily waived, if she had only asked.**

Would it be fair to say that this was a very expensive day for Joan? I bet you may be thinking that I should have jumped up from my desk, waved a white flag and begged Joan to come to her senses.
"Please ask me for a discount," I should have said?

I'm willing to bet there are people who would accuse me of not doing my job as a banker that day. Rubbish!

Here is a point that escapes the masses and causes them to stagnate in the bottom 80 percent group: *Bankers are paid to maximize profit!*

There was no time in my career when my boss called me into his office to say, "Look, Richard, we have met our quota for profit this month and so for the remainder, it's okay to give the farm away. Why don't you start deep discounting all of your mortgage business and make some of your clients really happy until I tell you to stop?" It never happened! Actually, the reverse would take place. I would be called upon to explain my actions in giving discounts to certain customers, no matter how well justified.

The bank, like any other business, wants to make a profit. It is all part and parcel of the central mandate of the financial institution to protect the interests of the investors. Nobody ever said anything about the borrowers!

In fact, in the past, there had been such shoddy treatment of borrowers by lenders that governments were forced to enact consumer protection laws. In Canada, we have "Disclosure Laws," and in the United States, "Truth in Lending." These are laws designed to regulate the behaviour of lenders to make sure the borrowers are made fully aware of all of the costs of borrowing. The politicians didn't just fall out of bed one morning and decide it was time to enact some consumer laws. What do you suppose was going on previously that would have caused the U.S. Congress to create a law with a name like "Truth in Lending"? They were responding to situations in which people were being taken to the cleaners by lenders of all stripes, including banks.

So it's buyer (or, in the case, borrower) beware. What else is new? My actions in dealing with Joan's mortgage renewal that day were perfectly in keeping with the policies of the bank. Even so, I must admit to some feeling of guilt as I generally did try and show my clients how to save money, a habit that had me in trouble more times than I care to count.

Here are some more examples of costly mistakes with mortgages. In very general terms, people make mistakes in:

- **shopping for mortgages**
- **setting up mortgages (deciding on the terms of repayment)**
- **applying for mortgages**
- **negotiating pricing on mortgages**
- **closing mortgages**
- **paying mortgages**
- **renewing mortgages**

Did I miss anything? Just about every mistake you can imagine is commonly made every day in every city, town and rural municipality in the country. I'm going to show you how to avoid the vast majority of these mistakes, and how to rescue, from the pockets of the big banks and other lenders, much of the interest you pay on mortgages and other borrowing products over a lifetime. Invest the difference wisely and you can amass a sizeable fortune!

A mortgage requires management, a financial plan all its own. I will show you how to manage it, but first you have to know how to acquire approval for low-cost mortgage financing in the first place. And in so doing, it may also be advisable to learn some of the traps and pitfalls mortgage applicants fall into that result in more time paying interest charges to the bank, unnecessarily.

-3-

Loyalty

"Had I but served my God with half the zeal I served my King, He would not in mine age have left me naked to mine enemies."
— *William Shakespeare, Henry VIII*

Loyalty is a wonderful virtue. Yet, there seems to be a dwindling amount of it in the world today, until you examine the relationships consumers have with the banks they deal with. Then there seems to be a never-ending supply of loyalty.

What causes people to become loyal to a given financial institution, so loyal that they would decide not to shop elsewhere for a mortgage and wind up paying excessive interest charges to "their own bank"? You may be surprised to learn that I encountered consumer loyalty practically ever day of my banking career and I still see it today in abundance.

In order to help you better understand the banking relationship and the effects it may have on the overall financial plan, the following describes a series of factors that contribute to loyalty.

The Familiarity Factor

Who knows you? The teller? The manager? What possible advantage could there be to being "known"? Perhaps it gives you a warm feeling to see familiar faces when you visit the bank. Are there any other benefits? If you're thinking that the fact you are known affords some sort of special privilege or consideration, I am sorry to disappoint you because it is just not the case. It doesn't increase your chances of getting a mortgage, nor does it have anything to do with pricing. You see, this "Familiarity Factor" is all one sided. It is a condition imagined in the mind of the bank client to create a feeling of comfort. I believe comfort is at the root of it and the cost of this fantasy is considerable.

Some clients have told me that they didn't think they would qualify for financing elsewhere because they were not known, that the new branch would have to see their chequing account operate satisfactorily for some time before a loan or mortgage could be considered. This statement is patently absurd. Being known is not a consideration in any credit decision. In fact, you may receive a more enthusiastic welcome down the street at the competitor's branch. Loans are approved or denied based on your ability and intent to pay, the collateral you have to offer and your assets. That's it!

Family Tree Factor

"Family Tree Factor" is the mistaken belief that because a family has dealt with a given bank since the days of the caveman, the bank should ante up with a perk or some kind of special consideration. Perhaps they should do something for the client they would not do for someone else who was just beginning their "Family Tree" relationship. Now I don't know how many generations it would take before you could expect to get something, but that's generally what "Family Tree" is all about. Let's consider John's story:

The Story of John

John wanted to buy a new car and needed a loan. He was very young, about twenty. He decided to approach ABC Bank because his dear father always made mention that he had been dealing with them going back to the end of the Second World War. John's father maintained a long-established record there, and besides, he owned a business and carried all of his accounts with ABC. John believed the bank would not dream of turning him down for a loan at the risk of his father moving all of his business.

John confidently sat down in the manager's office and proceeded to state his case.

"I would like to apply for a car loan."

"OK, have you applied for credit before?"

"No, but my dad has all his business here."

John expected a reaction. There was none.

The manager proceeded to take his application. Once finished, he just stared at it, hesitating. John became concerned. Then, believing he was about to be turned down, he decided it might be time to reinforce his father's importance to the bank.

"My dad's done business here a long time, with all of his personal and business accounts."

John thought this would send the manager reeling back in his chair.

Nothing.

The manager stared at John's application for a few minutes more, then said, "Will your father guarantee this loan for you, son?"

With his tail between his legs, John approached his father and got his agreement. He had learned that family history really had no effect on the bank, except perhaps to provide them with ways to further secure their loans.

Here is the reality check for the "Family Tree Factor": the records of your family's dealings with a given bank have no bearing whatsoever on your own dealings with that same bank. There are sometimes isolated exceptions made when the family may carry very large deposit balances. In these cases, politics rears its ugly head. However, on balance, "Family Tree" does not justify the extension of credit or the pricing of it. It may, however, afford the bank the opportunity to strengthen its position by asking for a family co-signer, as we have seen.

The Cradle Factor

"They have always taken care of me."

When someone says that they have always been taken care of by their bank, it seems to suggest that the bank, for some unknown reason, has gone beyond the call of duty to perform some kind of special service that was not really warranted. Perhaps it was more than was really deserved. This track record of successful experiences becomes logged in the mind of the bank client as a favour and translates into "they have always taken care of me." This could also mean that the client feels that the bank has never done them wrong, though this should hardly command the client's loyalty. The reality is that the client has just never made any unreasonable request of the bank that could have been denied.

The Seniority Factor

"I've been dealing with that bank for ten years."

The notion that the number of years one has dealt with a given financial institution has any bearing on anything at all is the most misguided judgement going.

Here's a brief story involving "The Seniority Factor":

The Story of Susan

Susan called me one day to announce she was selling her existing home and buying a new condominium. Susan was a new client, referred to me by another client of mine.

I visited Susan at her home to take her application and discuss what kind of terms she wanted. As we were talking, she began to tell me about the last time she applied for a mortgage. Apparently it had been a very frustrating experience for her.

"I went to my own bank last time. They wouldn't budge."

"They wouldn't take something off the rate for you? Your application is very strong."

"No, and I have dealt there for eight years. They said maybe 1/4 point, but only if I could prove I could get it somewhere else for that. They wanted it in writing."

"So what did you do?"

"I went to another bank and they offered me 1/2 of 1 percent off. I took it back to my bank and they said they would match it. I wanted them to beat it, but they would only match."

"Susan, why did you keep go back to your bank when it was apparent they were not demonstrating interest in keeping your business?"

"I've dealt there for eight years. I didn't want to change banks after eight years."

Dear Reader, it is my hope that you never, ever, subject yourself to the kind of humiliation Susan subjected herself to when she tried to maintain a banking relationship that was obviously of no importance to her bank. What Susan failed to realize is that her seniority of dealings with her bank was irrelevant. It is another example of a one-sided relationship, concocted in the mind of the bank client, of which the bank is not aware and could not care less about. Furthermore, Susan also failed to realize that it was not necessary to move her banking business in order to get a mortgage somewhere else. Had she wanted to keep her accounts with that bank (for what reason, I could not imagine) she could have done so and a new lender would have welcomed her with open arms.

Because of her one-way loyalty, Susan ended up paying a rate that was at least a 1/4-percentage point, and perhaps even 1/2-percentage point, higher than she could have qualified for somewhere else. This was all in the name of maintaining a long-term relationship that had stopped paying benefits to Susan a long time ago. Very tragic.

Here is the reality check for the "Seniority Factor": seniority of dealings with your bank has no effect in winning any type of concession or special consideration of any kind over any other bank client. You may well, in fact, win greater benefits as a brand new client somewhere else. Concessions are won on the basis of merit and negotiating skills.

Clearly, Susan would have been much better off if she continued shopping different lenders until she found one willing to give her what she wanted with no strings attached, and then given that lender her business. Her existing bank did not earn her repeat business and indeed did not deserve to, based on their performance.

I think there is a loss of self-esteem for the client when a situation like Susan's occurs. If you represent a good lending risk then you are a very desirable commodity to the mortgage market and most lenders would probably be willing to compete for your business. Wouldn't that make you feel better than sheepishly asking your bank to match someone else's offer? I think it would. You deserve better than that.

The We've Got 'Em Factor

The "We've Got 'Em Factor" is not an affliction of the client. No, this one belongs strictly to the bank and it may serve to explain the bank's actions in Susan's case.

The "We've Got 'Em Factor" occurs when the banker develops an attitude that once they have your business, they will never lose it. It causes the bank to fall into a comfort zone with your business, and once that happens, they feel free to take whatever advantage of you they want.

You may remember the first time you dealt with your bank. Perhaps you were warmly received and the bank made an aggressive effort to win your business. However, over the years the benefits you won have been disappearing. Suddenly, there are not as many perks as there used to be, and you find it more difficult to get what you want, even though your business has become more valuable and profitable for the bank.

You may say this is a terrible thing and wonder why your relationship has slipped over the years. Is the bank sending you a signal they no longer want your business? You may consider moving for a brief moment, but you suddenly check yourself. You consider how long it has been, perhaps ten years dealing there, and suddenly you become victimized by the "Seniority Factor". You find yourself hurting a bit, and frustrated, perhaps. Your ego is a bit bruised and you wonder what caused all this. The answer may lie in loyalty.

The bank can sense loyalty a mile away in a snowstorm. Their eyes and ears are open, and yours could be closed because of the aforementioned factors that serve to impair judgement.

Here is a prime example of the "We've Got 'Em Factor" at work. Although this one is not about banking, I will demonstrate its relevance for you.

Electric Typewriter

Many years ago, acting in my capacity as a branch manager, I was out for lunch one day with my boss and happened to mention that we needed a new typewriter. He said, "Buy it."

My boss was a man of few words. I thought I had won his concurrence too easily and added, "You realize I mean an electric typewriter."

"No way! They're too expensive. Get a manual."

A manual? This was the 1980s! As you may surmise, the company I was working for was not exactly on the cutting edge of technology. So, like a good soldier, I followed instructions and ordered a manual typewriter. When the bill came in, I nearly fell off my chair. It was over $700!

I telephoned a local typewriter shop to inquire about the price of an electric typewriter and found I could get a good one, fully reconditioned with a one-year warranty, for $300, far and away a better deal.

I began to investigate why it was my company had been ordering $700 manual typewriters. What I found was that we had one person in head office who was in charge of ordering business equipment. He had maintained a relationship with the typewriter company for over twenty years, knew the sales representative personally and, in fact, had begun to socialize with him on occasion.

The result of this cozy relationship was that over the years the price of the typewriters, which were automatically ordered from this supplier without checking market prices, had begun to escalate. The escalation went well beyond any inflationary effect, and it was abundantly clear that the supplier had been taking an increasingly larger slice of profit out of us virtually every time a typewriter was ordered. Thus, our company had been bitten by the "We've Got 'Em Factor," the payback for our unfailing loyalty of over twenty years. The judgement of our representative had indeed been impaired as a result of his loyalty and fraternization, and it cost the company a sizeable fortune. He had been ordering typewriters for a thousand branches.

As you can see, most anyone can fall victim to the "We've Got 'Em Factor" in any business relationship. It doesn't only apply to banking. Loyalty is the catalyst that sets the whole process in motion. Perhaps you now have a better understanding of a situation you may have experienced with someone you deal with, and I hope it will save you a sizeable fortune. No matter how cozy the relationship, it is always advisable to continually check the benefit of it against the market. Friendships and familiarity have no place in your banking relationship. Banking is a business, cut and dried.

Name-Brand Loyalty

Name-brand loyalty permeates the retail sector. Very often people make buying decisions based only on advertising, on images placed before them on television or some other form of media. However, name-brand loyalty, where consumer goods are concerned, can well be understood if the product has a proven track record. It just makes sense to go with a reliable product.

For example, I have found that Hewlett Packard makes an excellent product, based on my personal experiences with that company over the years. I know that any time I am in the market for a printer, computer or virtually anything Hewlett Packard makes, my investment with them will in all likelihood be a good one. Nevertheless, my decision to buy Hewlett Packard product is always based on a thorough review of the competition.

Now, it doesn't matter where I buy a Hewlett Packard as long as prices are comparable, and they usually are. I could buy it in any store in any city, town or municipality, virtually in any country on the planet, and enjoy the same degree of success with that product.

Banking is different. Banking is more of a service industry. They do have products like mortgages, credit cards and mutual funds. However, for the consumer to acquire those products, they have to rely on a certain level and standard of service that is much higher than required in a retail store. In some stores you can pick up your brand new Hewlett Packard printer right off the shelf and take it through the checkout like a loaf of bread, without ever encountering a salesperson. You cannot do that with your mortgage! Well, you can try, but you may find it difficult getting into the vault.

People often say, "I love ABC Bank. They give great service. Go to ABC Bank. They will take care of you." With this statement or belief, the consumer assumes that they will experience the same level of service with ABC Bank in any branch they visit. The branch at Main and Broadway, an excellent branch, will be the same as the branch at the corner of First and Second. Not necessarily!

It happens all the time, and you may have experienced this yourself. You have enjoyed a banking relationship for a number of years with a bank branch in your town. Maybe they have an excellent manager and the staff is very friendly and professional. It is possible. Then you decide to move to another city, and because you have had such wonderful success with ABC Bank, you decide to open an account at the branch closest to your new home.

Suddenly, all hell breaks loose. The manager is unfriendly — won't even give you the time of day. The lender is a moron. The employees keep their heads down as you approach the front counter, each hoping they will not be the one called upon to serve you. They wait until you have cleared your throat several times or rapped your fingers on the counter to get their attention, then they finally acknowledge your existence. You sense a definite feeling that your business is neither wanted nor appreciated.

What happened? How could two branches of ABC Bank be so different?

There is one key point you must understand, because not understanding it can cost you plenty. The level and quality of service you will receive from any branch of any bank, trust company or credit union depends entirely on the quality of manager and staff within that branch and their commitment to excellence. It has nothing to do with the brand name. Nothing!

All financial institutions have a policy, either written or not, to serve their customers well. There is very little difference between the policies of ABC Bank and XYZ Credit Union. Yet, the degree of customer service can vary a great deal. You could be standing in a perpetual lineup to get to a teller and notice a plaque with the company mission statement. Among other things, it pledges a degree of customer service unmatched in the industry. It just doesn't say which branch is providing that service. You obviously picked the wrong one!

There is a certain set of dynamics within any bank branch that affects the quality of service, and therefore product delivery to the consumer. It begins with the manager. No matter how much certain banks may try to deny it, the manager, his or her commitment to the job and his or her commitment to excellence will be the key-determining factor in the operation of that branch. Moreover, it all flows down through the chain of command through to every single staff member. If the manager is committed to excellence, he or she will not stand for anything less from their staff and will make sure they are consistently delivering quality. If the manager is weak, you will find that weakness permeates the entire branch, and you will feel it every time you come in contact with it, whether on the telephone or in person.

If you are faced with deciding upon a new bank branch to deal with, there is a good way to test the waters. Go there, having made the decision you are only shopping, and will not be making a buying decision that day. In other words, your banking business is up for grabs until you find a branch that impresses you. Leave all of your paperwork at home. Remember, the signage above the front door really doesn't mean anything.

Once you are there, be a visitor. Look around. Watch a customer approaching the counter where a clerk is present. Time it! Time it on your watch as to how long the customer stood there before being acknowledged. Remember, you're not there to buy, you are there to observe! Watch the customers as they interact with staff. Are they frustrated? Angry? Or, are they smiling, unequivocally happy as they leave the branch?

How is the atmosphere? Is it friendly? Tense? Intimidating? Cold? Professional? How does it strike you? Listen to the voices. Does the staff seem friendly and courteous? Are they making a concerted effort to help their clients? Do they seem to take a genuine interest? Look around! Is the branch professionally decorated or is it a dump? All these things matter. Perform your tests and observations in the context of being just a visitor. In order to appear inconspicuous, perhaps sit in the waiting area after wandering around a bit, read a magazine or a product pamphlet. Take some of the free information home with you to help with your decision. You are, after all, going to be buying, in the end, a product or service that could involve hundreds of thousands of dollars.

There is another test. How long has it been since you arrived? More than five minutes? Ten? Fifteen? Does it feel like you're sitting in the waiting room of an emergency ward? If someone hasn't approached you after a few minutes in the branch, it may be time to leave. Any competent and responsible staff member would have clued in by now that you are there, and they should be approaching you to offer their services.

Now, here is the final test. Ask to see the manager. Announce that you are a new customer, a potential customer, and you would like to meet the manager. Everything that happens from here will be crucial. Your announcement should trigger a succession of events all designed to make you feel welcome, wanted and appreciated. I will give you suggestions on how to handle your meeting with the manager in the next chapter.

Perform this test on at least three bank branches and compare your results before you make your decision. Please remember that anything less than excellence from a bank branch will carry a price. I would suggest that that is a price you cannot afford to pay.

-4-

Getting To Know Your Banker

"With a group of bankers I always had the feeling that success was measured by the extent one gave nothing away."
— *Lord Longford, British social reformer.*

Everything you have read so far, while it can significantly help your overall banking relationship, is really designed to prepare you in dealing with all aspects of your home mortgage, and other borrowing products that may affect it. You will not find advice on how to open a chequing account. I will leave that for some other author.

Preparation is of vital importance, especially in your dealings with mortgages. It is my intention to have you so well prepared that — if we use a baseball analogy — by the time you're ready to step up to the plate, you will be carrying a mighty big bat. You will, if you employ all of the principles I am about to teach you, hit the ball out of the park.

Getting to know your banker is a key aspect of your banking relationship and of your very financial success. Learning to deal with your banker will affect your financial future and will have a direct impact on how much interest you pay over a lifetime. There is no doubt about it.

Let's begin with your first meeting with the manager. Upon learning you are a potential new customer, the manager should respond very positively and welcome you with enthusiasm. Tell the manager right up front you are shopping around and are just trying to make your own evaluation of the branch and the products. You can ask about a specific product and ask the manager how it may be of benefit to you. He or she should engage you in conversation freely and in a friendly, non-threatening manner. It is also advisable to share with the manager the results of your review of the branch. That's beacause some managers are so introverted that they don't really know much about what is going on around them!

Now if you are so bold — and there is nothing wrong with doing this — as to share something that concerned you, like waiting too long, for example, and you do it in a positive, non-threatening manner, the manager's reaction will speak volumes.

If the reaction is negative, if you see a change in the facial expression of the manager, if his or her smile disappears as if a tax audit were just announced, you know you may have a problem. This type of banker will feel threatened by your observations and may very well resent the fact you had the nerve to survey the branch in the first place. It may well be that your interview will come to a very abrupt end after a series of brief and uninspired answers to your questions. You will be able to feel the negativity. If this happens, consider yourself lucky and move on. You may have just saved thousands of dollars!

If the reaction is positive, if the manager thanks you honestly and genuinely for your observations, you may well have discovered an excellent branch manager. A good manager sees a situation like this as an opportunity, not an assault against his or her integrity or ability. Good managers are expert problem solvers. In their eyes, a problem is an opportunity to acquire new business for the bank, to win a new customer. A manager who can do this with consistency is worth a fortune to the bank, to any company for that matter.

Now, why two different reactions? What was it that caused the first banker to react negatively and the second positively? This brings us to a key point in our discussion. If there is one word that could really describe what banking is all about, it is power.

If you will allow me to step outside my field of expertise for a moment, and give a personal opinion, I believe all human beings love power. I think they are drawn to it, whether they are willing to admit it or not.

Bankers are no different. They are power lovers. They are empowered with the responsibility of looking after millions of dollars of loans and investments. That has to be considered a power position.

I must tell you, for years I did not know what it was exactly that kept me in banking and finance. Yes, I enjoyed the work and it was challenging, some days more than others. I would sometimes end a bad day by asking myself, "What am I still doing in this business?" I would socialize with colleagues on occasion (in banking there are many occasions), say on a Friday night, and more often than not we would end the evening by discussing the business we were in. "Why are we in it?" No one could really answer the question definitively, though we would try. But just like a golfer who hangs on to the memory of a hole in one, I arrived at the course, uh, the branch the next day fresh as a daisy and ready to take some more abuse, loving every minute of it. I looked forward to the next time I would have that great and inexplicable feeling. Why?

One day, nearing the end of my career, I discovered the answer.

The Power Play

It was our Tuesday morning "sales" meeting. (The totality of what bankers know about sales could likely be placed on the head of a pin. They are just not well trained in that area.) One day, I became engaged in conversation with one of my colleagues about pending changes in bank operations.

We had been given authorization, within limits, to approve certain loans and mortgages. The bank was now taking this away, and giving the approval of loans to a central authority in Toronto.

This didn't really bother me as I had been through it before. If you're around long enough you see history repeat itself, over and over again, until you are so tired of seeing the same movie you have to go off and do something else, like write a book.

The changes did bother my colleague. In fact, he was really upset over it, and it was his next statement that finally allowed me to see the light of day.

"I can't handle the loss of power."

Well, I wheeled around on my heels to face him and to look into his eyes as he told me his feelings about this crushing event. Loss of power! Then he told me what he was doing about it, and to this day, while I know what I heard, I still cannot believe it.

"I'm refereeing hockey games."

"Excuse me, John?

"I'm refereeing hockey games in my spare time to help me get some of the power back."

Apparently, the decision-making power of a referee, the authority to make a call by which everyone must abide without question was a form of power replacement for John.

"What are you going to do in the summertime, John. Umpire ball games?"

"Yes, as a matter of fact. I've already signed up."

I could not believe what I was hearing, but it was absolutely true.

Power, for some people, can be intoxicating. John had had the power to approve or authority to deny loans and mortgages. This is one of the most awesome responsibilities given to people in banking. For some bankers, the sudden loss of this kind of power is debilitating, and they will look for ways to replace it. Some will also respond negatively to a loss of power.

Personally, I do not believe, as some would argue, that power always corrupts. I believe that power will corrupt corruptible people. Obviously, people who have power will either put it to good use or they will abuse it.

In banking, as you might expect, we have both types. I will call them Positive-Power Bankers and Negative-Power Bankers.

Let's return for a minute to our prior discussion about the two bankers. One was positive, the other negative, right? Would it interest you to know that those encounters were about power? They certainly were.

The first banker responded negatively to the client's boldness in surveying his or her branch, and then ended the discussion. Why? The client, by taking charge of the discussion and confronting the manager, however gently, posed a threat to that person's power. The client, in fact, robbed the manager of some of his or her power. It's that simple.

The second banker, our positive person, decided to use his or her power wisely, taking command of the situation in order to settle it to the client's satisfaction and win her business. This manager knew that the real, or best use, of power was to do good things, and get results that were pleasing to the client and the bank. That's win-win, the most desirable outcome to any business negotiation.

Now that we have discovered the two different types of bankers, let's take another look at our friend John. Can you tell by John's remedy for the loss of power what category he might fall into? Here's a story involving John:

Mr. Johnson

I received a call one day from our head office. They wanted me to contact a customer who had been shabbily treated by someone in another branch. I asked why someone else, such as the manager of that branch, could not take the call. They said the customer was so upset he didn't want anything to do with the branch or anyone in it, period.

I called the customer to get the story and see if I could help put out this fire.

"What happened, Mr. Johnson?"

"He hung up on me."

"Hung up on you? Why?"

"I don't know. I just wanted some information on early renewing my mortgage. Rates are down now and I called to see if I could renew and get a lower rate."

"Okay, that sounds reasonable. What happened next?"

"He came back to the phone after looking at my file and told me to just forget it. It wasn't going to happen because my penalty would be too high. Then, before I could say anything else, he hung up on me. Is that the way you treat your customers?"

"No sir, it certainly is not. Where are you now, Mr. Johnson?"

"I'm at home."

"Sir, can you give me fifteen minutes to look into this and call you back? I want to check your mortgage myself to determine if it would be to your advantage to early renew right now."

"Okay. By the way, I think his name was John."

"I know, Mr. Johnson. I know who it was. I'll take care of it for you."

When the call ended, I gained access to Mr. Johnson's mortgage file and found that it was indeed to his advantage to early renew. Mr. Johnson's mortgage was default-insured, and beyond its third anniversary, which, among other things, precluded the bank from charging any more than a three month interest penalty. Even with the penalty, Mr. Johnson would stand to save thousands of dollars.

I knew it was John who handled that call. It was his way. Just like a hockey referee, he had tossed poor Mr. Johnson into the penalty box. And John's word was final, or so he thought.

Imagine. Many people are severely intimidated by their bankers. I know for a fact that most people would have just let it go. They perhaps would have been angry at the way they were treated, but would not have thought to question John, being intimidated by his "power." John, in his haste to dump a call, was wrong, and it could have cost our client considerably. We ended up giving Mr. Johnson a sweetheart deal on his renewal. He deserved it.

I hope this chapter has helped you to better understand bankers. Just as in any industry, there are good and bad. Perhaps certain situations in the past in which you have been involved have now come into new focus. You will see, when we move on to mortgage negotiations, how this knowledge will help you neutralize the perceived power your banker may hold over you.

-5-

Debt

"A creditor is worse than a slave-owner; for the master owns only your person, but a creditor owns your dignity, and can command it."
— *Victor Hugo, Les Misérables.*

Debt, mishandled, will guarantee a lifetime of renting, paying someone else's mortgage. It will guarantee financial instability, even hardship. Debt can lead to some very unseemly consequences. It has been known to destroy chances, cause homes to be lost, shorten careers, wreck marriages and, in some extreme cases, even bring about suicide.

Now, debt is not all bad. Borrowing for a worthwhile purpose that one can afford, such as a home, is perfectly acceptable. However, borrowing money needlessly is a problem. Borrowing money needlessly is brought on by the desire for instant gratification, something which we have previously referred to as "The E Factor."

In order to understand where we are today with consumer debt let's first review a brief history. When I first entered the financial services industry in 1972, I remember that Visa was just starting to become popular. It had been around since the late 1960s, but it really started to take off in the 1970s. I can remember representatives from the bank coming into our offices at Friendly Finance one day, offering to pay us each $1 just to fill out a Visa application.

Before the coming of the major bank credit cards, people shopping in department stores would have to apply for a department store card if they wanted credit. Then, gradually, the department stores began to accept major bank credit cards as well as their own. Anyone looking for a small loan could try a bank, but at that time the finance companies were still the ones specializing in small loans. At Friendly Finance, we would have people lined up out the door starting around mid-November each year for loans for the

Christmas season. It was easily our busiest time of the year.

Whenever someone applied to us for a loan, we would take a new application, and reassess his or her ability to pay. This process allowed us to determine if someone was a candidate for credit problems because we could see a snapshot of their credit history from the last loan application forward. If they were too far in debt, and applying for credit too often, or for frivolous reasons, it gave us the opportunity to counsel the client and encourage them to curtail their borrowing until their debts were under control. Sometimes, when a client had borrowed elsewhere without our knowledge, and it came to our attention that they were having difficulty with payments, we would offer to "pool" their payments to creditors at no charge. "Pooling" was a process whereby the client would pay us a lump sum each month, and we would send amounts out to all their creditors in proportion to the amount they owed. This was a form of credit counselling, all part of our professional services.

So this process, whereby a new application and a new assessment were made for every credit transaction, really helped to keep things in check. It was a good service for the client even though most didn't realize it. In many cases it helped prevent people from suffering the very serious consequences of excess debt.

Credit cards changed all that. Credit was now being granted with a pre-established limit wherein the clients could self-approve a loan anytime they wanted to up to a certain amount. This was really the beginning of an unprecedented upsurge in consumer debt, as you may imagine. Without the benefit of professional guidance for each credit transaction, those most affected by "The E Factor" ran their finances into the ground with excess credit spending.

This less regulated form of lending was more profitable for the banks because they could charge substantially higher rates, e.g., 18 percent, than for personal loans, e.g., 12 percent, while their cost of money was exactly the same. This of course resulted in higher profit margins. Another factor in lending this way was cost. It was no longer necessary to pay an employee to reassess every credit transaction or to counsel a borrower. Thus, money was saved, and the process of reassessment was retained only for much larger and more profitable loans. This was just the beginning of good corporate citizenship giving way to the quest for higher profits.

As time passed there were more and more ways to access credit. The number of members in the credit bureau, i.e.: businesses extending credit grew by leaps and bounds as the retail industry enjoyed the benefits of the baby boomer generation in their most productive buying years.

By the 1980s a new form of credit card was emerging — the "private label" credit card. Here's an example. If you visit an electronics store — say, Acme Electronics — you may see a display of credit applications made to look like the store's own. However, if you read the application, you will find Acme Electronics is not the lender. The fine print may say that Friendly Finance is the lender, though the application and the credit cards themselves all bear the name of Acme Electronics. Thus the term private label. Retail stores found that it was cheaper for them to enlist the services of finance companies to run their credit card programs. After all, the clients were using the finance company's money and the store did not have to hire people to do the administrative work. Once again, more cost effective.

The private label credit card really reached its peak in popularity in the mid 1980s, with a credit program being made available to virtually any retail merchant who wanted one. Just as private label credit cards were gaining in popularity, and bank credit cards were also growing at a phenomenal rate, the baby boom generation reached its peak buying years and all hell broke loose. Thus, we came to call the 1980s the decade of excess because of all the spending that took place, much of it serving wants rather than needs. Every electronic toy imaginable was available to the public on open-ended credit programs (loans without credit reassessment), and it led to an unprecedented spending spree.

I can speak from experience about this period because, during this time, my job was to sell private label credit card programs to retail merchants. It was an easy sell. With so many merchants going into it, their competitors were forced to adopt this method of extending credit in order to compete. Once the market was saturated with card programs, retailers began to up the ante. They wanted to find a way to be different from their competition in order to attract business. They began to offer "interest-free" programs on their credit cards. This led to consumers spending even more because many of them operated under the misguided belief that if it was interest-free, it wasn't really debt.

In the beginning you had to make six or twelve monthly payments in order to get interest-free. Then, that evolved to three months without payment or interest, then six months, and finally some merchants were offering up to two years without payment or interest.

Can you imagine what happened to the people who were susceptible to "The E Factor"? They spun out of control! Some would make purchases with extended first payments, such as twelve months, and then forget about them. For many, it was as if they had acquired the merchandise for free, until the day of reckoning came when they were either forced to pay it all off in a lump sum, or refinance it over time with loans taken at exorbitant interest rates. Little did they know, they were mortgaging their future.

As the 1980s came to a close, I witnessed credit spending unprecedented in my career. There were some days when we were deluged with applications from just a handful of stores in a medium sized city. We were working overtime, sometimes Saturdays and Sundays to keep up and process it all. We would also attend sales promotions and offer on-the-spot financing, with our representatives on site, taking applications from buyers until midnight so that salespeople could spend more time on the sales floor earning their commissions. It was crazy.

I remember being appalled looking at the credit applications and credit reports of some applicants. There were many, I recall, who were applying at virtually every store in town. I could see everywhere they had applied because a record of it appeared on the credit bureau report. Every time someone applies for credit and a bureau report is requested, it's called an inquiry. It was not abnormal to see twenty to thirty inquiries within a three-month period on someone's record. Also evident was that these same people were beginning to show signs of being overextended with too much debt.

I knew that this borrowing trend, like all madness, would come to an end. In fact, I could see the end coming like a freight train barrelling down the tracks.

And then, abruptly, painfully, the end did come – it was the 1990s.

Something happened in 1990. It is difficult to imagine how things could be so good one decade and so bad in the very next. Maybe there is a rule of excess that says that the decade to come will be bad to the degree that the former was good. If that's true, we're in for quite a ride in the next ten years! In any event, it was and remains perplexing.

Corporations began to downsize in the name of becoming more globally competitive. People saddled with debt incurred from reckless spending in the 1980s, suddenly found themselves unemployed. One of debt's human qualities emerged: patience.

They learned, the hard way, that debt is very patient. It hangs around incessantly, testing the outer edges of your financial plan, until it senses a weakness, and moves in for the kill.

And move in for the kill it did. Many people not only lost their jobs, but some also lost their homes, unable to pay their mortgages on unemployment insurance. Since much of their disposable income had been going to service debt, they had no savings to fall back on. The divorce rate skyrocketed. Bankruptcies went to record levels. It was awful.

These are the insidious consequences of short-term thinking, of instant gratification, elements of "The E Factor." The bottom 80-percent of the population, in terms of financial standing, are affected by this condition to varying degrees while the top 20-percent seem to have more control over their spending. The 20-percent group seems to be able to recognize the difference between a want and a need, and is not easily swayed by advertising gimmicks, designed to appeal to their weaknesses. This group knows that poor decisions made today can have considerable long-term consequences just as they know that wise decisions can accumulate over time to pay substantial dividends.

I am certainly not suggesting that we all live our lives responding only to needs. After all, life is to be enjoyed, and I do think some people go too far in their thrift, amassing large fortunes that they never have a chance to enjoy. Can there not be a happy medium? Can't we live and enjoy life, while still saving for our later years? I think we can.

It's a matter of choice, I believe. Nobody forces us to incur debt. It's done at our own choosing. The choices we make in our youth, and in our middle years, accumulate to bring about a result in the later years. Sometimes the result is wonderful; it certainly is for those in the top 20 percent group. Sometimes the result is tragic; and for all too many this is the case.

There's a saying: "If you take a step forward, you can see enough to go further."

As we get older we can see our later years coming into focus (while just about everything else goes out of focus). I can tell you, at age forty-eight, I can now see sixty fairly clearly. I don't mind admitting it's a little scary. Suddenly the cumulative effect of the mistakes I made in my youth (and let's face it, we all make them)is looming. As is often said, regret weighs tons, discipline weighs ounces. "Had I injected the early disciplines, I would not be carrying such a heavy load." This is the lament of far too many people.

It's a tough way to learn, isn't it? The past cannot be changed. I have witnessed too many of the terrible consequences of debt, and I wonder why, as a society, we cannot seem to do better.

Education

I have had the good fortune to be blessed with two daughters. When my eldest was in university, she surprised me one day by mentioning she had acquired a credit card. I had no dreaming idea how she could qualify for credit of any kind since she was barely of legal age when she applied for it. She could not have demonstrated either the ability to repay, or the intent, having never borrowed money before. How, then, could any lender issue her a card?

This was when I realized that the banks were promoting their cards at the university level. Even though I was working in the industry at the time, I did not know what was going on and when I found out, I was furious. My anger was not directed at my daughter, but at the very industry in which I worked. It's one thing to offer credit to seemingly responsible adults, It's quite another to offer it to teenagers, many of whom are already financially stressed-out, trying to work their way through university.

I checked into it and found that there was a marketing philosophy at play. The banks were looking to land new customers by reaching them earlier in life by placing in their possession a high-profile product, a credit card. The banks had come to the conclusion that university students were very desirable potential customers because they would likely land good jobs (not a guaranteed proposition) and eventually accumulate substantial net worth. They were, in general, classified as better long-term prospects than those who did not attend university.

The banks also hoped that the card would act as an "anchor

product." They felt that a student with a credit card from ABC Bank would be more likely to continue their dealings with ABC in other areas such as full-service banking, mortgages and investment products. Every time a student would open his or her wallet and see the card, they would be exposed to the ABC name. Every time they received a billing statement, every time they wrote a cheque payable to ABC Bank, the name would become more internalized. This continued exposure, they hoped, would result in a lifetime relationship between the student and the bank.

The use of credit cards, especially among the young, especially those susceptible to "The E Factor," often results in a lifetime of overspending. The banks are aware of this, and of the likelihood that parents will bail out students that get into trouble with their cards.

Did your child take Financial Planning 101? Mine didn't, it wasn't offered. I find it completely inconceivable, considering the long-term consequences of financial mismanagement, that there is no effort to teach financial planning in our schools. Couldn't we find a way to give our youth the useful information they needed to help them fashion quality lives for themselves? I'm sure we could, and in my opinion, we should all work towards that end.

Credit-card issuers want cardholders to remain at or near the spending limit for most of their lives, until just before the ability to pay diminishes at retirement or loss of income. In this way, maximum profit can be achieved.

You will sometimes hear card issuers preaching responsibility and prudent judgment in regard to credit cards, while at the same time, dreaming up ways to increase card usage. This is not much different from the example of tobacco companies warning people of the dangers of smoking, while running ads targeted at youth. One product causes cancer of the body, the other of the bank account, which is slowly eaten away after years of abuse. Perhaps credit cards should come with warning labels just like cigarettes. Nonetheless, they represent financial dynamite in the hands of those not aware of their dangers.

I have no objection to lenders in search of profit. This is, after all, a free society. What I do object to is the manner in which we leave education about financial matters to the individual then inflict heavy penalties on those who mess up through ignorance. That is not a level playing field, and that must change.

Credit Card Incentives

I'm sure most people are familiar with the various credit card incentives in the marketplace. We are bombarded with information about them on an ongoing basis. But do they offer value? How much are these incentives really worth to us?

Everybody Pays

One day I was visiting my dry cleaner. We knew each other fairly well, as I was a regular customer and worked just across the way.

On this particular day my dry cleaner was not in a good mood. It seems someone had just taken him to the cleaners. He was grumbling that the bank had just doubled his discount from 2 percent to 4 percent. (The discount, paid to a bank by the merchant, is an amount *deducted* from the total of his credit card sales vouchers when he deposits them in the bank. For example, if the merchant had $100 in credit sales for a given day, the bank would pay $98 and keep the other $2. The $2 is the discount.) I asked him why the bank increased the discount.

"To pay for their frequent flyer program," he answered.

"What are you going to do about it?"

"Increase my prices. What else can I do? I'm not paying for people to fly all over the world."

"What about your competition?"

"They're in the same boat. Nothing is free. Everybody pays."

We are offered incentives to use credit cards but card issuers are recovering their costs from merchants, as well as from the interest they charge. We are encouraged to save "points" generated from credit card use as if we were accumulating a savings account toward a wonderful holiday.

Let's look at it another way. If you were a retail merchant and you were trying to decide how to price a given item, you would want to consider the cost of that item, plus whatever expenses you incur in selling it, plus your desired profit. The cost of bank discounts is a business expense for you. It is your cost for allowing your customers to pay you with credit. Would you not include the cost of bank discounts in making your pricing decision? Would it also be fair to conclude that those who pay cash and do not receive a discount on the price are subsidizing the cost of credit for everyone else? I'm willing to bet you know the answer.

I won't spend any more time on credit card incentives here. There are thousands of them, and they all follow the same general marketing approach. For the average consumer, these incentives are bad news as they are a factor in creating a pattern of overspending.

There are certain times when these incentives will be of value, such as when a business person deducts the cost of travel or is reimbursed by their company. Sometimes they are allowed to keep the frequent flyer miles they accumulate for their own personal use. However, these are the rare exceptions when card users benefit more than they pay.

Given what we have discussed so far, is it any wonder that so many people are in debt? We are living in a time where credit is more accessible than ever before. As I said, nobody forces people into debt, but they are seduced into it by some very powerful marketing devices. This where a huge gap exists between the knowledge level of consumers and lenders.

Interest-Free

Interest-free programs first came into prominence in the 1980s. They were used by merchants looking for new and innovative marketing devices to increase sales and deal with their competition.

Essentially, the merchants offered to pay the financing charges on a six-month or one-year purchase contract. The buyer would make six or twelve equal payments to a finance company, free of interest charges. But how? Finance companies routinely charged borrowers 24 percent interest!

Here's how. The merchant would write up the finance contract, for a $1,200 purchase with twelve equal installments of $100 and no interest. They would then sell the contract to the finance company. However, they would not be paid $1,200 for it. Instead, they would receive perhaps $1,080, $120 less. The $120 was the price the merchant had to pay to the finance company to "buy" the rate down from 24 percent to 0.

The discount amounted to 10 percent of the financed goods, a much higher discount than the 2 to 4 percent paid by credit card merchants. So, once again, how do you think the merchants paid for this discount? Did they allow the discount to reduce their profit margins below acceptable standards? Or, was the consumer paying for it in the price of the goods? Were those who were paying cash and not receiving a lower price consideration actually subsidizing the cost of the interest free programs? Common sense would lead you to the answer.

Interest-Reduced

Have you ever asked your banker for a loan at 1.9 percent to buy a new car? Did he or she fall to the floor, laughing uncontrollably?

Sometimes merchants will offer a substantially lower rate rather than interest free. Why? It costs less to buy the rate down to, say, 1.9 percent than it does to buy it down to zero. Make sense? Besides, 1.9 percent may actually sound more believable to an increasingly better-educated group of consumers than interest-free. Nevertheless, logic seems to elude the masses as they continue to bite on this sales hook.

In the final analysis, we all pay for the cost of credit in our society, whether we use it or not. Financial institutions recover the cost of incentives through the discounts they charge to merchants, along with the interest rates they charge to us. Merchants pass on the cost through higher prices. Like my friend the dry cleaner said, there is no free ride. Everybody pays.

Credit Cards

Credit card debt kills more mortgage applications than any other single factor, simply because monthly credit card payments, when they are added to the mortgage payment, interest and taxes can add up to an amount that the lender feels exceeds the ability to repay. In addition, the use of credit cards, the frequency of use and the tendency to carry balances from month to month acts as a barometer for lenders in evaluating your ability to take on a mortgage. Credit card abuse is a warning sign for the lender to stay away from a borrower who may not be able to handle credit.

I want to show you the payment record for a credit card account. Suppose you maintained a balance on your card of $2,500, with a 12 percent interest rate, and you were required to make minimum payments of 3 percent of the balance per month, a standard percentage in the industry. For the purposes of this example, we will say that you are just paying the minimum every month because that's all you can afford. In addition, you have decided not to charge anything to the card, ever again. How long would it take you to pay the balance in full? Three years? Five years? More? Take a look at the following chart:

Credit Card Balance of $2,500, at 12 percent Interest, Repaid By Making the Minimum Monthly Payment (3 percent of balance)

No. of Months	Payment Amount	Interest	Principal	Balance
Opening balance				$2,500
1	$75.00	$24.40	$50.60	$2,449.40
2	$73.48	$23.90	$49.58	$2,399.82
3	$71.99	$23.42	$48.57	$2,351.25
4	$70.54	$22.94	$47.60	$2,303.65
5	$69.11	$22.48	$46.63	$2,257.02
6	$67.71	$21.43	$46.28	$2,210.74
7	$66.32	$21.58	$44.74	$2,165.99
8	$64.98	$21.14	$43.84	$2,122.15
9	$63.66	$20.71	$42.95	$2,079.20
10	$62.38	$20.30	$42.08	$2,037.12
11	$61.11	$21.51	$39.60	$1,997.52
12	$59.93	$19.48	$40.45	$1,957.07
13	$58.71	$18.79	$39.92	$1,917.15
14	$57.51	$19.00	$38.51	$1,878.64
15	$56.36	$18.32	$38.04	$1,840.60
16	$55.22	$17.95	$37.27	$1,803.33
17	$54.10	$17.59	$36.51	$1,766.82
18	$53.00	$17.23	$35.77	$1,731.05
19	$51.93	$16.88	$35.05	$1,695.99
20	$50.88	$16.54	$34.34	$1,661.65
21	$49.85	$16.21	$33.64	$1,628.02
22	$48.84	$15.88	$32.96	$1,595.05
23	$47.85	$15.56	$32.29	$1,562.76
24	$46.88	$15.24	$31.64	$1,531.12
25	$45.93	$14.54	$31.39	$1,499.73

26	$44.99	$14.63	$30.36	$1,469.36
27	$44.08	$14.34	$29.74	$1,439.62
28	$43.19	$14.04	$29.15	$1,410.48
29	$42.31	$13.77	$28.54	$1,381.93
30	$41.46	$13.48	$27.98	$1,353.95
31	$40.62	$13.21	$27.41	$1,326.54
32	$39.80	$12.94	$26.86	$1,299.69
33	$38.99	$12.68	$26.31	$1,273.38
34	$38.20	$12.43	$25.77	$1,247.61
35	$37.43	$12.17	$25.26	$1,222.35
36	$36.67	$11.93	$24.74	$1,197.61
37	$35.93	$11.68	$24.25	$1,173.36
38	$35.20	$11.45	$23.75	$1,149.61
39	$34.49	$11.22	$23.27	$1,126.34
40	$33.79	$10.99	$22.80	$1,103.54
41	$33.11	$10.76	$22.35	$1,081.19
42	$32.44	$10.55	$21.89	$1,059.31
43	$31.78	$10.34	$21.44	$1,037.87
44	$31.14	$10.13	$21.01	$1,016.86
45	$30.51	$9.92	$20.59	$996.28
46	$29.89	$9.72	$20.17	$976.11
47	$29.28	$9.52	$19.76	$956.35
48	$28.69	$9.34	$19.35	$936.99
49	$28.11	$9.14	$18.97	$918.03
50	$27.54	$8.96	$18.58	$899.44
51	$26.98	$8.77	$18.21	$881.23
52	$26.44	$8.60	$17.84	$863.39
53	$25.90	$8.43	$17.47	$845.92
54	$25.38	$8.20	$17.17	$828.74
55	$24.86	$8.14	$16.72	$812.02
56	$24.36	$7.92	$16.44	$795.58
57	$23.87	$7.76	$16.11	$779.47
58	$23.38	$7.61	$15.77	$763.70
59	$22.91	$7.45	$15.46	$748.24
60	$22.45	$7.30	$15.15	$733.09
61	$21.99	$7.16	$14.83	$718.26
62	$21.55	$7.00	$14.55	$703.71
63	$21.11	$6.87	$14.24	$689.47
64	$20.68	$6.73	$13.95	$675.52
65	$20.27	$6.59	$13.68	$661.84
67	$19.86	$6.46	$13.39	$648.45
68	$19.45	$6.33	$13.12	$635.52
69	$19.06	$6.19	$12.87	$622.45
70	$18.67	$6.08	$12.59	$609.86
71	$18.30	$5.95	$12.35	$597.51

72	$17.93	$5.83	$12.10	$585.42
73	$17.56	$5.71	$11.85	$573.56
74	$17.21	$5.60	$11.61	$561.96
75	$16.86	$5.48	$11.38	$550.58
76	$16.52	$5.38	$11.14	$539.44
77	$16.18	$5.26	$10.92	$528.52
78	$15.86	$5.16	$10.70	$517.82
79	$15.53	$5.05	$10.48	$507.34
80	$15.22	$4.95	$10.27	$497.07
81	$14.91	$4.85	$10.06	$487.01
82	$14.61	$4.75	$9.86	$477.15
83	$14.31	$4.66	$9.65	$467.49
84	$14.02	$4.56	$9.46	$458.03
85	$13.74	$4.47	$9.27	$448.76
86	$13.46	$4.38	$9.08	$439.67
87	$13.19	$4.29	$8.90	$430.77
88	$12.92	$4.20	$8.72	$422.05
89	$12.66	$4.12	$8.54	$413.51
90	$12.41	$4.04	$8.37	$405.14
91	$12.15	$3.95	$8.20	$396.94
92	$11.91	$3.88	$8.03	$388.91
93	$11.67	$3.79	$7.88	$381.03
94	$11.43	$3.72	$7.71	$373.32
95	$11.20	$3.64	$7.56	$365.76
96	$10.97	$3.57	$7.40	$358.36
97	$10.75	$3.50	$7.25	$351.11
98	$10.53	$3.42	$7.11	$344.00
99	$10.32	$3.36	$6.96	$337.04
100	$10.11	$3.29	$6.82	$330.22
101	$10.00	$3.22	$6.78	$323.44
102	$10.00	$3.16	$6.84	$316.60
103	$10.00	$3.09	$6.91	$309.69
104	$10.00	$3.02	$6.98	$302.71
105	$10.00	$2.96	$7.04	$295.67
106	$10.00	$2.88	$7.12	$288.55
107	$10.00	$2.82	$7.18	$281.37
108	$10.00	$2.74	$7.26	$274.11
109	$10.00	$2.68	$7.32	$266.79
110	$10.00	$2.60	$7.40	$259.39
111	$10.00	$2.53	$7.47	$251.92
112	$10.00	$2.46	$7.54	$244.38
113	$10.00	$2.38	$7.62	$236.76
114	$10.00	$2.31	$7.69	$229.07
115	$10.00	$2.24	$7.76	$221.31
116	$10.00	$2.16	$7.84	$213.47

117	$10.00	$2.08	$7.92	$205.55
118	$10.00	$2.01	$7.99	$197.56
119	$10.00	$1.93	$8.07	$189.49
120	$10.00	$1.85	$8.15	$181.34
121	$10.00	$1.77	$8.23	$173.11
122	$10.00	$1.69	$8.31	$164.80
123	$10.00	$1.60	$8.40	$156.40
124	$10.00	$1.53	$8.47	$147.93
125	$10.00	$1.44	$8.56	$139.37
126	$10.00	$1.36	$8.64	$130.73
127	$10.00	$1.28	$8.72	$122.01
128	$10.00	$1.19	$8.81	$113.20
129	$10.00	$1.10	$8.90	$104.30
130	$10.00	$1.02	$8.98	$95.32
131	$10.00	$0.93	$9.07	$86.25
132	$10.00	$0.84	$9.16	$77.09
133	$10.00	$0.76	$9.24	$67.85
134	$10.00	$0.66	$9.34	$58.51
135	$10.00	$0.57	$9.43	$49.08
136	$10.00	$0.48	$9.52	$39.56
137	$10.00	$0.38	$9.62	$29.94
138	$10.00	$0.30	$9.70	$20.24
139	$10.00	$0.19	$9.81	$10.43
140	$10.00	$0.11	$9.89	$0.54
141	$0.55	$0.01	$0.54	$0.00
Totals	$3,617.10	$1,117.09	$2,500	$0.00

After 141 Months, Total Repayment $3,617.10

Are you surprised at the length of amortization? Were you close in your assessment of the length of time to repay the balance?

Why do you suppose it took so long? Was it the payments? The interest rate? Remember, this was based on an interest rate of only 12 percent per annum! Can you imagine how long it would take at 18 percent? Let's just say a good while longer.

The reason it took so long is because of the small payments set at a fixed percentage of the declining balance.By making the minimum payment the borrower stretched out the time required to pay off the balance. Of course, had there been any additional charges placed on the card along the way, it would have changed the whole picture. Using an example like this, it's easy to see how card balances can remain with us in perpetuity.

The opposite effect, reduced amortization time, can be achieved by making payments in excess of the minimum required amount. The rate of reduction with slightly larger payments can be just as amazing as the rate of increase in amortization with slightly smaller payments. Therefore the interest savings with larger payments can be dramatic. When we look at that difference on a mortgage, as we will later, the outcome will dazzle you! This is preparing you somewhat for a concept I will introduce in the next chapter that you will find truly amazing.

To illustrate the effect of higher payments and lower amortization, the following table demonstrates how a loan of $2,500, the same amount as the aforementioned credit card balance, would look over a two year period even at the *ridiculous* interest rate of 33 percent per annum.

Loan of $2,500 at 33 Percent Interest, Repaid with fixed payments over 24 Months.

No. of Months	Payment Amount	Interest	Principal	Balance
Opening balance				$2,500.00
1	$140.99	$64.45	$76.54	$2423.46
2	$140.99	$62.48	$78.51	$2344.95
3	$140.99	$60.45	$80.54	$2264.41
4	$140.99	$58.38	$82.61	$2181.80
5	$140.99	$56.25	$84.74	$2097.06
6	$140.99	$54.06	$86.93	$2010.13
7	$140.99	$51.82	$89.17	$1920.96
8	$140.99	$49.52	$91.47	$1829.49
9	$140.99	$47.16	$93.83	$1735.66
10	$140.99	$44.75	$96.24	$1639.42
11	$140.99	$42.26	$98.73	$1540.69
12	$140.99	$39.72	$101.27	$1439.42
13	$140.99	$37.11	$103.88	$1335.54
14	$140.99	$34.43	$106.56	$1228.98
15	$140.99	$31.68	$109.31	$1119.67
16	$140.99	$28.87	$112.12	$1007.55
17	$140.00	$25.97	$115.02	$892.53
18	$140.99	$23.01	$117.98	$774.55
19	$140.99	$19.97	$121.02	$653.53

20	$140.99	$16.85	$124.14	$529.39
21	$140.99	$13.65	$127.34	$402.05
22	$140.99	$10.36	$130.63	$271.42
23	$140.99	$7.00	$133.99	$137.43
24	$140.99	$3.54	$137.43	$0
Totals	$3383.76	$883.74	$2500	$0

Please compare the totals in this chart to the totals in the preceding chart. What do you find? The total interest paid is $883.74 on the loan versus $1,117.09 on the credit card, *$233.35 less,* even though the rate is 33 percent on the loan versus 12 percent on the card.

This is an example that there is something more to the cost of a loan or mortgage than just the rate itself. That something is time.

Am I advocating that you borrow from finance companies? Certainly not. I am using this comparison as an example of how preposterous it is to borrow from credit cards and to only make the minimum monthly payments. In the case of someone who has incurred so much credit card debt they cannot afford to pay more than the minimum payment, this comparison demonstrates the insidious consequences.

Many times during the course of my career, people have told me they began using credit cards when they were very young, and over time they had never been able to fully repay the balances. They had just kept charging until the cards were at, or near, their limits.

Consider a case in which someone maintains a $5,000 card balance at 18 percent interest from age twenty-five until retirement at sixty-five. (Believe me, it happens!) What's the result? The individual would pay a total of approximately $72,000, at $150 per month for 480 months (forty years). That's bad, but consider this. If that same individual found a way to pay cash for purchases, and invested the $150 a month at an average rate of return of 8 percent per annum, compounded annually, by age sixty-five he would have accumulated approximately $486,000!

It's true. You can literally pay the equivalent of your retirement nest egg in debt payments, and be left with nothing at the end of the trail. It happens far too often and I wanted to show you this to emphasize the long-term financial hardship that can result from the misuse of credit cards, as well as other kinds of debt.

Car Loans and Leases

After credit card debt, car loans and car leases are the second most common deterrent to fulfilling the dream of homeownership. Often they work in tandem with credit card debt to destroy the chances for mortgage approval. Some mortgage applicants tend to make major automobile purchases right before they apply for a mortgage. The resulting car payment often blows their chances to secure that mortgage. The applicant is then relegated to renting for a while, perhaps even years, until his or her debt is brought under control. What is the effect of this delay in becoming a homeowner? It can derail the implementation of a of a sound financial plan for years, and result in tens of thousands of dollars in lost equity.

I can well identify with the desire in one's youth to purchase the first new vehicle. It's overwhelming. The automobile companies heavily advertise and design products in order to appeal to all market groups. With the aid of computer mailing lists and partnerships with credit card companies, these groups are targeted with laser-like precision.

Included in the advertising is, invariably, an "E Factor" carrot, some kind of inducement to demonstrate that the product can be easily acquired. In the case of cars, that inducement seems to usually involve purchase by monthly payment.

Let's discuss the monthly payment for a moment. If we consider a $30,000 vehicle purchased with 20 percent down, the payments over 48 months would be $617.45 at 11 percent per annum compounded semi-annually, not in advance. That's with a $6,000 down payment! Over 36 months it would be $782.96 and over 24, $1,115.87.

Today, most consumers, especially those in their early working lives, would not be able to afford such a payment and still have their own place to live, whether they are renting or buying. If looking to buy a home with a monthly car payment of $782.96, a buyer earning $30,000 per year would only qualify for a monthly house payment of $217.04, taxes included! Have you seen any $6,000 homes for sale lately? Are there any $200 apartments for rent in your area?

So the automobile companies have a problem. They can see that the cost of cars represents a much larger bite out of the average income today than it did before, and that is a threat to their very existence. So, a means had to be devised to make the vehicles more affordable, that means is leasing.

Want to rent your car forever? Lease it! The lease is just a fancy rental contract with a smaller monthly payment that goes on in perpetuity as you change vehicles. That is, unless you decide to pay the residual balance at the end of the lease term and buy the car, which often entails an ill-afforded loan anyway.

While car payments take a large bite out of the average consumer's budget, they can also play havoc with a mortgage application, especially if credit card debt is also present.

So what's the answer? Can't people afford cars anymore? Well, it all depends on where you want to go with your financial plan. A new car every three or four years can very well mean the difference between living a retirement in comfort or in quiet desperation. So, the message here is buy if you must, and buy what you can realistically afford, only after you have deducted the 10 percent you pay yourself. If you begin to pay yourself before major purchases happen, and gauge your ability to pay for those purchases with the remaining income, then you will be well on your way to a bright financial future. However, if you try saving after you are already in debt, you may find you have gone too far and there won't be anything left to save.

Perhaps a two or three year old car is right for you. Today the trend is to keep cars longer. Much longer. Drive through any newer neighbourhood. I'll bet you will find some very nice homes with clunkers parked out in front. Times have changed. Where two car families were very common twenty years ago they are not today. In fact, the combination of a new home and a new car for the average Canadian family is probably no longer affordable. The house and the car just do not seem to go together for anyone other than those in the upper income groups who tend to be in the top 20 percent. Those in the bottom 80 percent of wage earners who attempt to keep up usually wind up in trouble.

Does your budget tell you that you can only afford a ten-year-old car? Buy it! You may not want to go around showing it off, but you may also find yourself better off down the road than your show-off friend who was concerned with "image." Short-term gain. Long-term pain.

If you are planning on purchasing a home, and the purchase of a car is to precede it, make sure you will still be able to afford the home.

Here is some advice I can give you with respect to the use of credit cards and the purchase of automobiles, the two deadly factors that prevent homeownership.

Friendly Tips

• **You should never carry credit card balances for more than sixty days. If you do, it is a sign you have entered a deficit-spending trend and a warning to get things under control. Some experts maintain that those who cannot pay their monthly card balances are technically bankrupt.**

• **When you are deciding to apply for a credit card, ignore the questionable incentives they offer. In fact, in all probability, the more incentives, the higher the real cost of the card. Opt for a card with a low regular interest rate in case you incur charges, together with low or non-existent transaction charges. If you exercise prudent judgement, you will be able to afford to pay for your next plane ticket instead of relying on your card issuer to buy you one with your own money. Remember, the incentives are there to grab your attention and to draw it away from the true cost of the card. They're just smoke and mirrors.**

• **When you receive your credit card, read the cardholder agreement word for word. You are bound by the terms with the first usage of your card. It helps if you know them and you may find negatives that were not disclosed in the up-front advertising.**

• **After making a credit card purchase, deduct the amount from your chequebook balance. (You do keep a running chequebook balance, don't you?) This way you can tally the entries and write a cheque at the end of the** month for the sum total of all your credit purchases. You will be less likely to carry a balance forward because you'll be living on the remaining income after credit purchases have been reimbursed. You will have better control this way. This suggestion came to me from one of my past clients.

• If you purchase a car before a home, and plan to buy a home before the car is paid off, you must be careful. I would recommend you see a competent lender first to get a pre-approval letter for a mortgage in the price range of the home you will be buying.(I'm jumping ahead a bit because we will be covering pre-approvals in a later chapter.) Tell the lender you are planning to buy a car and ask how large of a car payment would be allowable give the price range for your home. Get at least two estimates on this as lenders do make mistakes on pre-approvals, as we will see. Then, allow yourself 75 percent of that recommended car payment in order to factor in a comfort margin.

• If you buy a car after the home, which is what I recommend, you still have to be careful with affordability. You don't need to crowd your ability to make the mortgage payments. Always try to assess your own affordability level, which will invariably be on the conservative side of what most lenders will allow. (We'll discuss analyzing your own financial ability to pay for credit in a later chapter). You'll stay financially healthy that way.

• If you're paying cash for a piece of merchandise, bought from a retailer who is running an interest-free program, negotiate a cash discount for yourself of at least 10 percent of the purchase price. Tell them you know they pay a discount to a bank or finance company and that you don't want to be subsidizing the cost of credit for everyone else. I'm willing to bet you'll have a very surprised retailer on your hands.

• Sleep on it! If you decide to wait until the next day to consummate a purchase, you will find that in most cases, your desire to purchase a given product will dissapear. If it does not, that is a sign the purchase, if affordable, may well be warranted.

-6-

The Credit Report

"A man's indebtedness... is not virtue; his repayment is. Virtue begins when he dedicates himself actively to the job of gratitude."
— *Ruth Benedict, The Chrysanthemum and the Sword.*

In this chapter you will learn, among other things:

• **The importance of obtaining a copy of your credit report before your lender sees it.**
• **How to identify and correct negative information on your credit report that could jeopardize your credit application.**
• **How lenders share information about you.**
• **How negative information, not attributable to you, can find its way onto your report without your knowledge, and what you can do about it.**
• **How your credit rating can decline even as you are paying your bills on time.**

Did you know that virtually every credit transaction you make is electronically tracked? Every loan and mortgage request, every credit card transaction, every payment you make and every payment you miss; every cheque you bounced; every dispute you may have with a retailer – even that speeding ticket you forgot about? That's correct, it's all tracked and made available to your lender in a summary form called the credit report.

To say that the credit bureau report has an impact on your plans to become a homeowner is the understatement of the century. There was a time many years ago when the credit report wasn't nearly as important as it is today in the decision-making process for a mortgage lender. These days, if you want to be a successful mortgage applicant, you had better be able to prove you are ready for credit sainthood, or you may find yourself renting for life!

(I want to mention here that I don't believe you are somehow cursed if you rent. Renting a home can be a sensible financial descision under the right circumstances. Certainly there are those who can save for retirement very well without ever becoming homeowners. However, I believe they are in the minority.)

When I started out in the financial services industry, the credit bureau compiled information manually. Today, I can plug my laptop computer into a telephone line in my client's home, use the modem to dial up the credit bureau, and have the report on my screen in a matter of seconds. We have certainly come a long way.

With this close monitoring of "credit behaviour," lenders are now able to track your habits with a great deal of precision. It was once possible to miss a payment or two, and have the lender not report it out of goodwill; now, computers share all your information. You can't sneeze without it showing up on your credit report, and this is weeding out many mortgage applicants who would have qualified under the old system.

There is another method, used by lenders and credit bureaus alike, to evaluate the credit performance of an individual and assess their worth as a lending risk. This facility is called credit scoring.

In 1974, I welcomed some visitors to my office at Friendly Finance. They were sent by our parent company in the United States to review loans, all types of loans. They wanted to see good loans and bad loans. They wanted to evaluate open loans and loans that had already been paid off.

In the course of their review they looked at many factors. Which income groups had bad loans? Were teachers more apt to pay their loans on time than say, truck drivers? Who was more likely to incur too much debt, doctors or secretaries? If a person had been employed at the same job for a long time did that represent a better risk factor?

All the data collected was fed into a computer and out came a scoring system, a numerical evaluation given to a credit applicant based on the factors of employment, income, length of residence and credit history. This numerical information was subsequently shared with other companies who were willing to pay for the research. What emerged was a system that, for the most part, is today virtually unchanged throughout the industry.

The credit score was initially used as a guide to help point out weaknesses in a credit application, to help the lender make a more accurate decision. Today, the credit score is the decision-maker. If an applicant scores beneath a certain cut-off value, they don't stand a chance of being approved. Many companies have a policy that the credit score can be overridden by a human decision in order to allow for flaws in the computer's judgement, of which there are many. However, lenders tend not to do so for political reasons: they fear reprisal from their employers if overridden loans suddenly go bad.

A major flaw in credit scoring evaluation is that computers make no assessment of how the information got there. None. If the lender is not willing to intervene, an unjust decision can result, as they do on a daily basis, all over the country.

Here's an example. Let's say someone lost his or her job due to downsizing. As a result of lost income they can no longer pay their obligations. They immediately start looking for a job, all the while reassuring their creditors everything will be fine. It takes six to nine months to find work, and once employed again they resume payments, bring everything up to date over, say, three to six months, and continue paying their obligations faithfully, just as they always have.

Someone else is an habitual credit abuser. They are late every month regardless of their income. They lack the intent and the will to pay on time. They treat their credit as if it was a right, and they constantly complain about creditors "hassling" them for payments.

Would you like to know what the great tragedy is here? Viewed through the eye of a computer, these two credit reports are treated exactly the same way!

The credit report of our downsized friend, who has spent a working lifetime building up his or her credit, will look like a train wreck and they will be given a low score, probably below cut-off. In this manner, the downsized person is given the same treatment as the habitual credit abuser. That, my friends, is wrong.

The penalties for poor credit history, no matter how the information got there, are very severe. Each instance of a reported negative rating has a life expectancy of six years. That's right. One mistake can haunt you for 6 years because the credit bureau keeps a record of it for that long, no matter how good the rest of your history is.

Now, this brings us to another downside of technology. There are times when bad information can be reported about you without your knowledge.

You may suddenly find it difficult to obtain credit. Perhaps a credit card company rejects your application based on information received from a credit-reporting agency. You wonder how that could possibly be. You're a credit saint, never made a late payment in your entire life. You're upset and understandably so. You decide to investigate (Don't just let it go, dear reader!) and you call the credit bureau to obtain a copy of your report. When it arrives, you stare at it in disbelief as you find something there that is not attributable to you at all. To illustrate, here is a case study:

The Story of Steve and Kristin

In my business — I suppose in any business — you do not always meet nice people. However, on this occasion, I was fortunate. I received an Email from a very wonderful couple, Steve and Kristin. They had taken a stroll through my web-site and were interested in perhaps transferring their mortgage away from the credit union with which they were dealing. They had been impressed with a mortgage renewal strategy I shared with visitors to my site (and one I will share with you later on).

I arranged to meet with them in their home one evening. I liked them instantly. They were professional people, teachers both. As we sat down to discuss their mortgage, Kristin served a brew of flavoured coffee made from beans she ground herself. I can still taste it!

Steve and Kristin began to tell me their story. They had been married for about four years, and lived in the home Steve had previously shared with his former spouse. Kristin had never been married before. In taking their application I found they were excellent candidates to receive a very low rate on their mortgage renewal. They had good jobs, good income, very little debt and at least 25 percent equity in their home. They were quality people all the way, and I was very motivated to work hard to find them the best mortgage deal in town.

When I returned to my home office, I performed my usual first task: I dialed into the credit bureau and requested a report, fully expecting theirs to be clean. I would then send it up the line, and ask the lenders to bid for the business of this outstanding couple.

I was then very surprised to find that though Steve's credit file was fine, Kristin's looked like a train wreck!

It appeared at first as though there was nothing I could do for Steve and Kristin. I stared at the report in disbelief, thinking I had just been duped by a very wise credit abuser. How could it be? Was my judgement about people so unreliable after all these years? It didn't add up.

I knew there was something wrong with this report, having seen these kinds of things happen before. But what? After a short time, the answer came to me. This report painted a picture of someone who abused credit by failing to pay credit card obligations to airline companies. She was a world traveller, it seemed, a frequent flyer, and she took people for a ride everywhere she went! There was a litany of bad faith credit dealings for which you might expect someone could be sent to jail. The report also painted an opposing picture of the same person who had paid the remainder of her obligations faithfully for years. This person was more like the person I had met. Confident that there had been a mistake, I decided to have another visit with Steve and Kristin. I had to. There was no other way I could win a mortgage approval for them.

I did not give them my reason for the next meeting, only asking for their time, and they agreed. I had to be careful about the manner in which I approached this, not wanting to offend them. As we sat down once again with some of Kristin's excellent coffee, I asked, as if walking on eggshells, if they had ever heard about anything negative on their credit report.

Steve and Kristin both looked at each other with surprise.

"We thought that was all taken care of " Steve said.

"That came up a couple of years ago," Kristin added "I started to get calls at work, people trying to collect bills I didn't owe. They used my maiden name and I told them I had since been married. I gave them my birth date and social insurance number, but they continued to insist these were my debts. I tried to convince them I was not the Kristin Waverly they were looking for. They conceded that our birth dates and social insurance numbers did not match, but since the information appeared on my credit report I had to be responsible for it."

"What happened next, Kristin?" I uttered this question with a sense of newfound relief.

"Well, the calls would come and go. I went to my bank one day and they suggested I call the credit bureau, which I did. I tried to convince them but I don't think they believed me. They just said they would take care of it. I told my bank manager about what happened and he said I shouldn't worry about it. I thought I could just forget about it, until today."

It was obvious that Steve and Kristin were not only genuinely concerned, but angry and frustrated as well. Their reaction to the news confirmed for me that they were being sincere, and that they were in fact the excellent people I had first judged them to be.

I verified every piece of information on that credit report with them, and I determined that the negative content indeed belonged to someone else. I told Steve and Kristin that this bad information would have to be cleared before I could present a mortgage application to a lender. I told them it could take up to two weeks and that I, as a member of the credit bureau, would have a better chance of success than they would as consumers. The bureau is extremely wary of information supplied directly from consumers, simply because they have heard just about every lie in the book. Here is where professional representation would really help.

I was successful in having all the negative information removed from the report within five days. The credit bureau was sceptical at first, but I helped them to identify another file in their possession that was the actual file of the credit abuser. Somehow, by the similarity in names, the computer system had wrongly merged the two files together and dropped the identity of the credit abuser, making it look like it all was Kristin's information.

My next visit to their home was a happier one. I presented Kristin with her new credit report. She and Steve presented me with a thank you card and a bottle of fine spirits in appreciation for what I had done.

Armed now with one of the finest applications a lender could ask for, I did win that great deal for Steve and Kristin. They transferred their mortgage and won all sorts of additional perks as well.

This was a prime example of how information can swirl around computer systems and mistakenly wind up on your credit report, causing all sorts of grief.

We have now seen how bad information, not belonging to you,

can find its way onto your report and pose a threat to your credit application. Is it possible that good information about you will not find its way your credit report? Could that be as bad? Worse?

The Story of Jennifer

Jennifer was in the market to buy a home. She had just relocated from another province after divorcing her husband of many years. She was looking to start a new life and to purchase a home she could share with her daughter, a university student.

Jennifer decided to call the toll-free number of a major bank to apply for a mortgage over the telephone. She thought it would be more convenient, and besides, the bank was offering some incentives she thought were of value.

The bank representative took her application, an exercise of filling in the blanks, and pulled a credit report.

"I'm sorry, we cannot authorize your application."

Jennifer was very shaken by this answer.

"Why?" she asked.

"You don't have any credit, and because of that, your application fails to meet our scoring requirements."

"But I do have credit. I have a bank card and a department store card. I pay them faithfully."

"Madam, the credit report says you do not have a credit history."

"But…"

"I'm sorry. There is nothing more I can do."

With that, the conversation ended and it looked as if Jennifer would be forced to rent a home. She didn't want to do that. She had owned before and was well aware of the importance of a home in building a financially secure future. Dejected, she told her real estate agent about the experience and he called me.

I found that Jennifer's credit report was indeed missing some information. I believed Jennifer when she said she did have credit cards that she paid faithfully. But why were they not summarized on the report? I called the credit bureau and gave them Jennifer's credit card numbers. They found that Jennifer had had two files created for her under different addresses. Jennifer had moved, and for some reason, a separate file with her new address had been created but contained none of her credit information.

The credit bureau agreed to merge the two files into one consolidated credit report with all the necessary information on it. Then I applied on Jennifer's behalf for a mortgage. She won an approval for her mortgage from the very same bank that had previously turned her down.

What went wrong here? The bank representative Jennifer had dealt with was either not experienced enough, or did not care enough, to listen to a sensible story. Furthermore, he may not have known what to do about it anyway. Instead, believing that the credit bureau's word is gospel, the rep preferred to believe Jennifer was lying.

This sort of thing happens all the time. Is it the fault of the credit bureaus? Not necessarily. Overall, they do a pretty good job of organizing information. However, the information they receive is input by thousands of credit grantors of all kinds. If the information is input incorrectly, it can severely alter a credit picture, as we have seen. At the same time, some lenders have a tendency to blame everything on the credit bureau, the computer or anything else they can find rather than accept responsibility for a negative decision. I believe it all boils down to power: "If I am right I retain power and if I am wrong I lose it to the client. Therefore I cannot run the risk of being wrong. Therefore I will blame others." Unfortunately, this is the thinking of some.

There is something terribly wrong with the credit system that I must discuss. You will recall in the chapter on debt we talked about education and the role it could play in helping young people to identify marketing techniques aimed at getting them into debt. I believe education is also required with respect to credit reporting issues.

Consumers are asked to play by the rules of the credit system, which are there to protect the interests of investors. There's nothing really wrong with that. The problem is consumers are never properly told what the rules are. They may know some of the rules by common sense or by trial and error. Nevertheless, despite the absence of a formal education process, consumers must pay a substantial price for any mistake they make with credit.

I am willing to bet there are some credit rules you know nothing about. Did you know that...

- **You can lose credit points if you apply for credit too often within a short period of time?**
- **You can lose points if too many of your credit cards have been opened recently?**
- **You can lose points if your credit card balances are commonly at, or near, your spending limit, the very place the card companies would like you to be?**
- **That you can lose points if you owe money to a finance company?**
- **That you can lose points if you have very little, or no credit history?**

All of the aforementioned examples of ways to lose credit points have something in common. They have nothing to do with the manner in which you pay your obligations. You could be the most honest and sincere person on earth, a credit saint, and should too many of these factors come into play, your application could be rejected without you ever having missed a payment!

Here is another thing you need to know: *rejections breed more rejections.* That's correct. Your chances of being rejected again increase with each new rejection. That's why it's so important to get it right the first time. Some lenders, if they see an inquiry from another lender, will automatically assume you were turned down. Their logic is that the other lender must have had a good reason for rejecting your application and, rather than investigate themselves, they just turn you down. You could have been only shopping or you could have been turned down unjustly. No matter. Rejections can, and do, breed rejections.

These factors have nothing to do with prompt payment but they have everything to do with other kinds of credit behaviour. That is why credit scoring is also sometimes referred to as behaviour scoring.

Used by many lenders and credit bureaus, behaviour scoring relies solely on the behaviour patterns that appear on your credit report. For example, if you have applied for credit too many times recently, you can be automatically judged by the scoring system as a borrower out of control, a person with bad intentions applying all over town for credit. Instead, you could have been shopping for a car. Perhaps you went to several dealerships and they all checked your credit before you found a deal you liked. Those credit inquiries are seen by the system as negatives and points are deducted.

You can lose points for dealing with a finance company. Banks view someone dealing with a finance company, even if only to establish credit after being declined by a bank, as a less than ideal candidate.

You may also find yourself dealing with a finance company without even knowing it, and lose points that way. Remember the private label credit card merchants? Finance companies often operate their credit programs. Well, now you know that something as innocent as financing a television over three months with no interest can cost you your credit score. If you were close enough to the cut-off value at a time when any of the aforementioned factors came into play, that could be enough to torpedo your mortgage application.

Now that you are aware of these factors do you have a better understanding of how you should *behave* with respect to credit? Wouldn't it be nice if consumers were informed of the rules they are expected to follow? Instead, they remain a guarded secret until the unsuspecting consumer applies for credit and then the rules are hauled out of the closet and used as a facility for denial.

As you can probably tell, I am not a fan of automated scoring systems. I believe they are discriminatory and result in unjust credit decisions that hurt people. They also give the financial institutions an unbelievable amount of control over lending. You might say that automated scoring is a good thing for them, and it would be, if it were always used properly. But that's just not the case.

Bankruptcy

It used to be that bankruptcy was only for poor money managers, business failures and credit abusers of ill intent. They were the ones most likely to be bankrupt.

Today, that has changed. As a result of downsizing in the 1990s we have seen a growing classification of bankruptcies – those who have always paid their bills faithfully, but lose the ability to do so due to tragic circumstances. They lost their jobs, and in many cases, they have lost their homes as well.

I have no quarrel with the penalties that people who abuse credit must pay. I still believe proper education would prevent much of it. However, I believe it's unjust to apply these penalties to those who were forced into bankruptcy by factors they could not control, such as the economy.

I believe we should apply newer, more socially responsible rules to these people and give them a chance to re-enter the economy as productive citizens. For them, a six-year sentence of credit denial is hardly a fair response.

Today, only a handful of financial institutions will consider someone who once was bankrupt for a mortgage, even though mortgage default insurers will cover them after two years discharged. In most cases, these institutions have a blanket policy against lending to people who once were bankrupt no matter what factors caused the bankruptcy in the first place.

I have colleagues in the United States who tell me that bankruptcy is not looked at with the same degree of scorn as it is in Canada. In the U.S., people are more likely to get a second chance and I believe we should do the same. I do not believe in tossing good people onto the scrap heap. That has social consequences for all of us and besides, it is just plain wrong.

If you have become bankrupt because of circumstances such as downsizing, try not to be discouraged by the negative treatment you may receive at the hands of others. Remember, the system was originally set up to break the fall of good people. Unfortunately, it has been abused like all social safety nets. Hold your head high and take heart, it's not the end of the world. In fact, you could look at it as a new beginning.

To conclude, I am going to share a few more things with you that should help in your quest towards good credit and the rewards it can bring:

Friendly Tips

• **Never go more than one year without obtaining a copy of your credit report in order to make sure the information it contains is accurate. If you don't understand the report, most credit bureaus will provide assistance.**
• **Never apply for credit, especially a mortgage, unless you have already seen your credit report and have had a chance to correct any erroneous information.**
• **Always pay your debts on time, including credit cards,**

unless there is an interruption in your income that reduces your ability to pay. In the absence of loss of ability, wrongful intent is assumed, and it can have devastating consequences.

• The fact that you have failed to pay your $59 department store account for three months because it is "insignificant," in combination with behaviour patterns, can ruin your chances of being approved for a mortgage or any other type of credit. Everything matters! This fact does not escape most people in the upper 20 percent group.

• If you do have problems paying your bills, approach your creditors directly and immediately to discuss a solution. Arrangements can usually be made in cases of a temporary loss of ability. The best results are gained through negotiation with a decision maker within the institution. Running or avoiding the problem will only cause your creditors to haul out the big artillery. You don't need that.

• When shopping for a car, a mortgage or anything else requiring a credit application, obtain a copy of your credit report and bring it with you to show the lender or merchant. In this fashion they should be able to tell you whether or not you will qualify without their having to do their own inquiry to the credit bureau. This will minimize the number of inquiries on your file and help you save those precious credit points.

Now that you have been introduced to the way credit is reported, and to lender requirements, you probably have a good idea as to how your own application would be received, at least with respect to your intent to repay. But that is only part one of a two part scenario. Your *ability* as well as your *intent* to pay must both be in evidence to qualify for credit. In the next chapter I will discuss how to assess your own ability to pay *before* you see your lender.

-7-

How To Self-Qualify for a Mortgage

"The human species, according to the best theory I can form of it, is composed or two distinct races, the men who borrow and the men who lend."
— *Charles Lamb, Essays of Elia.*

In this chapter, among other things, we will discuss:

- **How lenders assess your ability to pay a mortgage.**
- **How you can assess your own ability to pay before you see a lender.**
- **Why you should beware of the affordability test used by lenders.**
- **Why your income source may or may not be acceptable to lenders.**

We will be looking at a few charts, so you may want to buy yourself a copy of the mortgage payment tables. You can buy one at most any bookstore. However, if you don't have one, that's fine, as I will do the calculating for you.

Before I show you how to qualify yourself for a mortgage, based on your ability to pay, it may be helpful to demonstrate how the financial institutions do it. Then, you can compare your own results to theirs. I must warn you in advance that sometimes the results of the lender's affordability test and yours will not be in agreement. You may believe you can afford a certain home, while the bank disagrees. Alternatively, you could also find the lender approving your mortgage for more than your own figures indicate you can afford. It all depends on your personal financial situation.

Let's use the following figures for our example:
- **a mortgage of $100,000**
- **a five-year term**
- **a 25-year amortization**
- **a rate of 7 percent per annum (compounded semi-annually, not in advance)**
- **payments of $700.42 per month**
- **property taxes of $1,800 per year, or $150 per month**
- **heating costs of $75 per month**
- **total family income of $42,000, or $3,500 per month**

The first test of your ability to pay such a mortgage is called the Gross Debt Service ratio (GDS). The GDS ratio is your housing expenses expressed as a percentage of your income. It is calculated like this:

Mortgage payment (principal and interest) + taxes + heating costs + 1/2 monthly condo fees, if applicable, over your monthly income

Therefore, $700.42 + $150 + 75 = $925.42, or 26.43% of $3,500

The current guidelines call for a maximum GDS of 32 percent. So this mortgage is within the affordability of the applicant under the first test.

The next test of ability to pay is called the Total Debt Service ratio (TDS). The TDS ratio is your housing expenses plus your consumer debt payments expressed as a percentage of your income. It is calculated like this:

Mortgage payment (principal and interest) + taxes + heating costs + 1/2 monthly condo fees, if applicable + all consumer debt payments, over your monthly income

Let's say our applicant had the following debts:

- **a bank loan for $250 per month**
- **a bank credit card payment of $100 per month**
- **a department store credit card payment of $25 per month**

The TDS calculation would then go like this:

**$700.42 + $150 + $75 + $375 = $1300.42,
or 37.14% of $3,500**

Currently the maximum standard for TDS is 40 percent. So, we know that this family meets the income requirements under the second test. As long as they have limited debt, the required down payment and steady income, they will most likely be approved for a mortgage.

This is a rather simple test you can perform on your own financial situation to determine affordability. You must remember we are dealing with only the lender's guidelines here. These basic guidelines (32 percent for GDS, 40 percent for TDS) have been around for many years with very little change.

However, there is a problem. Society has changed. There was a time when we would only use the income of the primary wage earner in the family. Then we began to use half of the other spouse's income and finally we were using it all. It was becoming more and more difficult for families to make ends meet, and for many of them this meant both spouses had to work.

As time marched on, increased taxes and other inflationary factors, took an increasingly larger bite out of the average family budget. Despite this, the affordability guidelines remained largely the same.

Some years ago I began to take a look at this problem. It dawned on me that, by using a fixed percentage of the gross as a comparison, we were ignoring the fact that net income was constantly being eroded by expenses. In performing my own analysis on a test most bankers widely accept out of habit and tradition, I began to wonder why we never took into consideration how many children were in the family. Having been awakened to child-rearing costs as a father, it seemed strange we didn't factor in whether there were two children in the family or ten. We weren't looking at childcare costs, which in day care alone could easily run from $200 to $400 per month per child.

I soon arrived at the conclusion that the differences could be fairly substantial and that there was a chance we could be giving people mortgages they could not really afford! These affordability tests could be way off the mark and completely out of touch with modern-day reality.

A Day of Reckoning

A client visited my office one day with a very worried look on his face. He apologized for not making an appointment but I assured him his timing was just fine. Very nervous and concerned, he began to tell me that he was having trouble making his mortgage payments. In fact, for the first six months he had been borrowing from his family to cover the shortfall. I immediately wondered, as all lenders would, if we had missed anything when we approved this mortgage. After all, we had nothing to gain by placing someone into a home they could not afford.

I spoke to the man briefly, asking him several test questions, all of which he answered to my satisfaction. I then decided to pull his file and to go through every detail with him. All our file information was correct. There were no debts we did not know about, his income was as he said it was and our calculations had been done correctly. His TDS was 37 percent. While this was slightly high, it was still fine according to the accepted standards. We advanced mortgages with these same set of numbers all the time. How could he possibly be having trouble making the payments?

I decided to do a budget with the client right there in my office. I wanted to know every single expenditure he had. When we had finished, we found that based on his actual take home pay versus his total expenditures, he was about $500 short of breaking even. I have since forgotten what expenses caused the budget deficit, but it was little wonder, once we saw the figures, that he found himself borrowing from relatives to pay the mortgage, even though he had very few debts.

Unfortunately we were not in a position to do anything for the man. The payments were as low as they could be and he was faced with a decision to either sell the house or find other sources of income. He decided to sell the house. Not a pleasant experience.

Dear reader, please take my advice and *never* enter into a financial agreement someone else says you can afford. Only you can determine affordability, based on your own knowledge of your true expenses. What do you spend on food, clothing, travel, insurance, entertainment, day care and all other expenses unique to your situation? How much do you allocate to savings? Add it all up and then calculate the maximum shelter payment you can afford. Only then will you know for sure, though you may find yourself at variance with what your lender is telling you. It's not that lenders are trying to mislead. It is just that they are going through a process given to them as a matter of policy. These are merely tests, not accurate representations that can be relied upon to address all situations.

Before we move on, I want to make one final point about affordability evaluation. During the course of my career, I noticed that the vast majority of mortgage applicants would enter into a home purchase transaction with very little if any idea as to the impact that transaction would have on their budget. Most, in fact, did not have a budget at all. When it came time to try and figure out if they could afford a specific mortgage payment, for those who actually performed that calculation, there was no consideration given to monthly savings. Consequently, borrowers would often buy the most expensive home they thought they could afford, or that the bank would approve, and would become house poor the day they moved in.

When you calculate affordability for a mortgage or any other kind of debt, you must include savings, the payment you make to yourself each month, in your TDS calculations. In other words, you must consider yourself a creditor. You owe a debt to yourself. That debt is the total amount it will take to sustain you in retirement plus whatever additional money you will need along the way for those rainy days, vacations and other expenditures. Needless to say, it's a big debt and it does require regular monthly instalments. If you choose not to take that into account, you run the risk of over-mortgaging yourself and running your budget off the rails.

Being house poor is no laughing matter. Homes require maintenance. Taxes go up – very regularly, I might add. The furnace fails. The water heater bursts. The winter wind blows half the shingles off your roof and you have a $500 deductible to pay. It all costs money you may not have budgeted for. You could find yourself in a deficit budget situation every month, just like the client I talked about earlier. Some people may not even realize there is a problem, unconsciously allowing the deficit to spill over onto their credit cards each month. When the cards are maxed out, the day of reckoning arrives. This is the great dilemma for far too many homeowners.

The following is a hypothetical scenario involving a couple who wish to buy a home, comparing their actual family budget to the bank's affordability evaluation. The results are sobering.

The Story of Michael and Cheylene

Here are some initial facts about our home buying couple:

- **Michael and Cheylene sold their first home and used the equity to buy a new home for $175,000.**
- **After a 15 percent down payment, they signed a mortgage for $151,725 at 7 percent over 25 years. The monthly payments including taxes and heat are $1,387.**
- **They both worked and had two children in day care.**
- **They each travelled fair distances to work so they needed two cars.**

Their net income and expenses are detailed in the following chart. The expenses are conservative estimates. Please remember, home prices, insurance rates, property taxes, utility rates and other expenses vary across the country, so an average was used.

Item	Monthly Expense Income	Net Monthly
Total Net Family Income from Two Wage Earners		$3,900
Mortgage, Taxes & Heat	$1,387	
Car Payment	$350	
Credit Card	$150	
Department Store	$25	

Food	$600	
Clothing	$200	
Insurance for		
Two Cars	$200	
Car Repairs		
& Maint. Est.	$150	
Home Insurance	$40	
Miscellaneous	$100	
Entertainment	$100	
Hydro	$100	
Telephone	$50	
Cable	$45	
Water	$30	
Day Care	$400	
Sub Total Expenses	$3,927	-$3,927
Funds Left Over		-$27
Savings	?	
Life Insurance	?	
Home Maintenance	?	
Medical & Dental		
(Not Covered by Insurance)?		
Vacations	?	
Final Budget Deficit		???

If you look at the subtotal the budget is clearly in the red, even before a multitude of other expenses people commonly forget about are considered. We have not even included a factor for what I call "budget leakage," a term everyone should be able to identify with.
Is this family in trouble? You bet they are! Their deficit, whatever it is, will spill over and result in an increased debt load which will in turn increase payments to service that debt. Thus, their financial situation will get worse every month until the Spam hits the fan, so to speak.

How did the bank approve this mortgage knowing the budget situation of Michael and Cheylene? The fact is they knew very little about it and used an entirely different calculation to measure affordability. Here is the industry-standard affordability test for Michael and Cheylene.

Total Family Income Before Deductions	$5,450
PITH (Principal, interest, taxes & heat)	$1,387
GDS (Maximum 32%)	25.45%
Total Debt Payments	$525
Total Monthly Outlay	$1,912
TDS (Maximum 40%)	35.08%

Given that the income was reliable and proven, the credit was good and the equity from the sale of the previous home going toward the down payment, most any mortgage lender would have approved this deal in a New York minute! Now perhaps it is easier to see how my client of many years ago found himself in a home he could not afford.

I don't want to discourage you. I just want to point out you must be careful when entering into a financial transaction of this magnitude. The financial institutions do not have all the answers. You must take the responsibility to make sure you can afford whatever it is you are buying and still reserve funds for *you* every month!

Developing the discipline to pay yourself first does not always come easy. One mortgage client of mine considered himself a creditor. He had maintained a $400 monthly allocation to mutual funds and had amassed over $30,000. He and his wife thought they had found the perfect home for themselves until they visited my office one day. When I told them what the payments would be, they looked at each other and announced it was too much for them. Such a payment would jeopardize their $400 allotment to mutual funds each month and so they decided to look for a less expensive home.

This was a couple who had it all together. They had absolutely committed themselves to a financial plan and they had the inner strength to say "No" to the temptation to place it all in jeopardy with an unwise house purchase. I have no doubt that today they are living happily in a modest home they can afford and are well on their way toward a retirement in comfort with all the peace of mind that brings.

Income Sources

I mentioned earlier that income had to be deemed reliable to be considered. There are different guidelines for the various income groups and here are some of the more common ones (please keep in mind that these and all rules are subject to change):

Those Employed by Someone Else:
• **Generally speaking, you must have completed at least one year at your current job, or be able to prove a continuous history of employment in the same occupation for more than one year.**
• **You must not be under probation at your job.**
• **Your income is considered without overtime, unless you can prove overtime hours are a regular occurrence (you will be asked for tax return information to prove this). However, if you are relying on overtime to qualify, you are probably buying too much house!**
• **Part time income is usually only considered if it can be proven to be regular, just like overtime.**
• **Casual income is not usually considered (but there are exceptions).**
• **Income from multiple jobs is considered on a case-by-case basis. There are too many variables to discuss, but generally speaking, if your second job is taking you beyond forty hours a week you should think twice about relying on it to pay your mortgage.**
• **Documentation acceptable to the lender will be required in the form of letters of employment verification, T4s and/or pay stubs.**

Any Portion of Income Derived from Commissions:
• **Most lenders, with rare exceptions, require a three-year track record of earnings.**
• **Income for the three years is averaged to arrive at the allowable income for debt servicing calculations.**
• **Only net income after expenses is considered.**
• **Three years' tax returns and notices of assessment are usually required as proof of income.**

Self Employed Applicants:

- **Three years' track record of earnings is required.**
- **Income for the three years is averaged to arrive at the allowable income for debt servicing calculations.**
- **Some lenders will only count taxable income.**
- **Three years' tax returns, notices of assessment and financial statements are usually required.**
- **Some lenders will look at taxable income plus some reasonable "add backs" like depreciation and other expenses which are unique to the borrower's situation.**

So far, we have reviewed the general guidelines for income qualification. You should now be able to perform your own assessment of your income qualifications using first, your own personal budget, and then the affordability test used by lenders. In most cases, if your own budget calculations say you can afford the payments, the lender's tests will also result in the affirmative. If they don't, there could be something wrong with your own budget calculations.

Credit Qualification

As we discussed in the previous chapter, your credit score, or behaviour score, will very possibly make or break your mortgage application.

You will not be able to assess your credit report with the same degree of accuracy you measured your income qualifications. First, the credit bureau will not divulge the credit score to you or tell you exactly what individual evaluations are given to each point. We can only talk about points in general terms to help you have some idea as to how this will all turn out and how strong your application will look to a lender. Second, though you may score in the acceptable range, the lender can still choose to decline your application. So, the score is not as automatic an approval mechanism as it is a denial mechanism.

Let's start from the top. (By the way, many credit bureaus now use everyday language in the reports they send to consumers. These reports will be formatted differently from the report the lender sees. Nevertheless, the essential information should remain the same.) You should see your name, address, former addresses, place of employment, former employers, along with other personal information like birth date and social insurance number. Check all of this information for accuracy. Any information not belonging to you should be removed by the bureau, as its presence represents a danger that someone else's credit information has found its way onto your report.

Next, there could appear items of public record like judgements, collections, or records of bankruptcy. We hope not, because these items will all seriously reduce your credit score. Once again, if there is anything here not attributable to you or inaccurate, you must discuss it with the credit bureau and attempt to get it resolved *before* you see a lender.

If there are any paid judgements and/or paid collections, make sure they are shown as paid on the credit report. Some companies are notorious for not reporting paid items. If this is true in your case, go after that company with the credit bureau's help. In the lender's eye, a paid collection is one thing, but an unpaid collection raises all sorts of red flags!

There are times when a collection registered in your name can be a surprise. Here's an example. Say you buy a vacuum cleaner from a department store and you have trouble with it. Perhaps you have a dispute with the store, and you arrange to settle your charge account for 50 cents on the dollar. This is the store's way of satisfying your concerns. So you pay the 50 percent and the store writes off the rest. The store then decides to send a report to the credit bureau which effectively says that you refused to pay 50 percent of your balance. This will show up on your credit report as a "settlement." Lenders view settlements in the same way they do bad debts. Negatively.

Whenever you are engaged in a dispute or some other action that you know will manifest itself on your credit report, it is incumbent upon you to weigh the factors. Is refusing to pay the amount that would fully satisfy the creditor's claim worth the damage it will inflict on your credit history? You would be amazed how many cases there are where people have stood steadfast on principle on a $50 disputed debt, only to pay penalties many times over. Do you really want a disputed debt to have to be factored into a decision on your mortgage, a transaction involving hundreds of thousands of dollars? Please remember, a little item may well, in combination with other things like a couple of late payments, drive your credit score below cut-off.

I am not suggesting that you pay any claim a creditor makes as ransom against a bad credit report. There are times when a matter is worth fighting for. Just weigh it on sensibility scales before you take the gloves off and decide to punch yourself right in the nose! It is possible, when negotiating a settlement, to reach an agreement that the creditor does not report the matter to the credit bureau. If they won't agree to that, your own common sense should come into play.

If you have a bankruptcy on your credit report it is not the end of the world, as most lenders would have you believe. If you are putting less than 25 percent down, under current guidelines from mortgage insurers, you may qualify after being a minimum of two years discharged from bankruptcy. Yet, many lenders ignore this consideration and automatically decline former bankrupts. A few will look at it on a case-by-case basis and we are thankful that they will because as we have discussed previously, not everyone becomes bankrupt the same way.

If you are formerly bankrupt and are less than two years discharged, you may well have to come up with 25 percent or more down. This is just a reflection of the increased risk lenders believe you represent. In these cases they most often follow their own guidelines, instead of those written by mortgage insurers.

In addition to the two years discharged requirement, some lenders will also look for signs of re-established credit. People often ask how they can re-establish credit when no one will grant them any. It's a fair question. One idea is a secured credit card. You simply plunk down $500 or $1,000 of your own money to be held as security, and the bank issues a credit card, if they are satisfied with your application. If you default, the bank cashes out the card with your deposit. A secured credit card is a good way for people who once were bankrupt to regain a satisfactory repayment record.

The next aspect of the credit bureau report we will discuss is the repayment history. This is where the rubber meets the road, so to speak. Your report will likely show every credit dealing you ever had, except mortgages, unless you deal with credit unions that are reluctant to report their loans to the bureau. The report will show instalment loans, those on which you pay a fixed monthly payment, as well as revolving loans like credit cards and lines of credit where you can reborrow under a set limit. Since the reports sent to consumers are now written in everyday language, it should be easy for you to understand what your creditors are saying about you.

If your accounts are all showing paid without incidence of lateness, fantastic. This will really help your credit score. If the report shows cases of slow payment beyond one month, you may be in for trouble. The scoring systems of today are very unforgiving, and with respect to repayment history, you really do have to be a "credit saint" not to lose points.

There are so many possible situations and combinations of good and bad ratings that we could never cover them all here. You can, however, make sure that whatever is reported is accurate. If you see something in the report you don't agree with, get it resolved. If a payment has been reported late and you have a receipt indicating it was paid on time, do not let it go. The impact could be too costly to your credit score, especially when we consider that many lenders use scoring to set pricing. That's right, your mortgage rate may be a product of your credit score. Like I said before, *everything matters*!

One final point. If after looking at your credit report you are discouraged, please do not turn yourself down. It may well be worth a visit to your bank or your mortgage broker to see if the lender can find a way to justify a loan for you. It's a fact that most lenders dwell on the negative and look for ways to turn people down. Nevertheless, there are still enough lenders who operate from the positive side and will give it their best for you.

The Property

Yes, after income and credit, the property is the final qualifying factor in the process. You could have the best credit in town and a high income with no debts, but if the property does not conform to the lender's or the mortgage insurer's policies, then you do not have a chance of being approved. The property is the security the lender holds in case your ability to pay the mortgage diminishes. Thus, it is of paramount importance. Well, somewhat important. Slightly important? Please allow me to explain.

For high-ratio mortgages (less than 25 percent down) which require mortgage default insurance, it used to be a requirement that the home be appraised by a qualified appraiser. The role of the insurer was to approve the property using the appraisal report and the role of the lender was to approve the applicant (on behalf of the insurer) based on income and credit qualification. Consequently, buyers found comfort in the fact that the insurer had approved the property. Rightly or wrongly, they considered it a good sign.

The tide, however, is changing. Insurers, like most corporate entities, hell bent on increasing profits through expense reduction, have begun to rely on an automated process. Instead of direct appraisal, they assess the property using historical data from their computers, and other factors. In essence, this means the inspection of the home by a qualified appraiser is, in most cases, no longer required.

I believe, and many of my colleagues believe, that taking the appraiser out of the loop is not a positive thing. Who is to attest to the condition of the home is in today, except for the buyer who is not a qualified expert. With a some of the safety margin eliminated from the process, the possibility of buying a home with a serious latent defect increases. That is, unless the buyer decides to spend $300 or $400 or more on a home inspection, which may not include an appraisal of the home's market value. In this fashion, the insurer has shifted more of the burden onto the buyer. Yes, the computers make the approval time faster, but we seem to pay a price for that just as we do with automated credit scoring.

To review what we've learned in this chapter on self-qualification:

Friendly Tips

• **Before applying for a mortgage, go through the process of self-qualification. You will be much better prepared when you meet the lender, and you will reduce your chances of a nasty surprise.**
• **Order your credit report as well as your proof-of-income documents well in advance of your meeting with the lender, so you will be sure to have them in time and with you at the meeting. You would be surprised how much this speeds up and smoothes out the process.**
• **Use your own family budget as the first test of the affordability of your mortgage. Don't rely solely on the lender's assessment of your ability to take on the mortgage.**

• Always maintain your personal records in pristine order. Things like missing pay stubs and T4s and incomplete financial statements can delay the process while sending a negative message to your lender.

• Any inaccurate information appearing on your credit report should be addressed before your lender sees it.

• You should have a detailed explanation ready for the lender to cover any incidence of late payments. Make sure your reasons are credible – lenders have heard them all, and a fairy tale will only serve to dig a deeper hole.

• Bring as much documentation with you as you can to prove your case. Letters from creditors, paid receipts and credit card statements can be useful tools in casting aside any element of doubt.

• Order your own appraisal. I have always made it my policy, when buying a home, to order an appraisal report for myself, separate and aside from any report ordered by the lender. I believe it is money well spent because the appraiser is working for me, not for the bank, and I am therefore better assured I'm not overpaying for the house.

Please note there are always cases of exceptional circumstances. In these cases common sense dictates that the special considerations be made, and lenders are empowered to make them.

-8-

How Lenders Market Mortgage Products

You and I are almost ready to go shopping for a mortgage. However, before we can do that, I want to show you how to tell the difference between a silk purse and a sow's ear. That's figuratively speaking, of course! There are many different mortgage products in the marketplace and very often, particularly in the spring, they go on sale. You should be able to recognize and place the correct value on them.

Mortgage Gimmicks

For a moment, I would like you to imagine yourself as a retail storeowner. You decide that you want to have a promotion to help create buyer interest and increase sales. For this promotion, you will want to select a few products for "special" pricing. Perhaps you've received a discount from a supplier that you want to pass on to the public. Perhaps you have an existing product that you want to present in a different way to make it look "new" or better than the same product offered by the competition. People have always been fascinated with the words "new and improved."

So, you want your products to be or appear less expensive than the same products offered by the competition, while maintaining a reasonable profit. If you price your product too low, without any room for negotiation, you could stand to lose money on a large percentage of your sales. That's why the best solution would be to create the appearance of newness to satisfy the appetite for new, and to package the product in such a way that it only *appears* less expensive than the same product offered by your competition. You could decide to throw in a couple of perks you bought for cheap which don't really affect your profit very much but stimulate buyer interest, because they are free. Free is another good word in marketing. People know nothing is really free, yet the idea of getting something free still attracts crowds. It's a proven business stimulator!

Somewhere along the line the financial institutions caught on to these basic marketing philosophies. Bankers began to ask themselves, If they can do it in the automobile industry, why can't we do it in banking? If they can sell furniture this way, why can't we use the same approach to sell mortgages?

And they did! Soon there were so many "new" mortgage products on the market it was impossible to keep track of them. The lenders could all see through the window dressing of these marketing campaigns, but borrowers, particularly first timers, were being caught up in the fish nets like you wouldn't believe! Since they didn't have the training to see through all the smoke and mirrors and to calculate the real value of these programs, they paid for it dearly.

You see, falling victim to a gimmick when buying a toaster is not the same as falling victim to a gimmick when looking for a mortgage. If you lose a couple of bucks on the toaster, so what? But if you lose tens of thousands on the mortgage and wind up with years of additional payments because of it, that's an entirely different story.

One advantage to having gimmicks is that they draw the buyer's attention away from features of the product itself, or from the idea that the product could be had for a lower price. The buyer focuses on the gimmick, and since most of the attention is paid there, other factors, possibly very disadvantageous ones are ignored. The gimmick creates the impression that the buyer is getting the best possible deal available, and that causes him to go to sleep.

Mortgage gimmicks have exactly the same effect. They tend to put the client to sleep with "benefits" that appear to be utterly fantastic, yet when viewed under a microscope and dissected, have very little benefit at all. They may, in fact, have exactly the opposite effect and may not be in the best interests of the borrower; mortgage gimmicks may actually result in years of additional payments!

Before we move on from here and disscuss the specific mortgage gimmicks or "incentives," as they are known in the mortagage market place, I want to give you a visual image that may help you look at marketing in a different way.

Imagine a very large, round serving tray laden with wonderful-looking gourmet delights. The food is arranged by type in rings all around the tray. In the outer ring, the one that's most easily reached, are the goodies–desserts like cookies, cakes and pastries,which make your mouth water. As you look farther in towards the centre, the next ring may have breads – fresh-baked and delicious. In the centre and a bit of a reach away, are vegetables, low fat proteins like lean chicken and fish and other nutritious foods.

You could look at the mortgage market in much the same way. The outer ring of the market contains the so-called goodies – the gimmicks. They are within easy reach and taste wonderful. People gobble them up. The more they eat, the more they want. Yet, a steady diet of them can lead to devastating consequences. In fact, people eat so much of the outer ring, by the time they get to the centre where the really nutritious food is, they don't have any room for it. That is exactly what the restaurant owner, or mortgage lender, wants.

The goodies are cheap, the nutritious food expensive. If you fill up on the cheap food and pay a nutritious food price, the restaurant makes more money. Similarly, the mortgage lender wants you to grab the goodies (the gimmicks) and run, thinking you have hit the jackpot while the lender makes a killing keeping the good stuff locked away.

Cash Back

I don't know what is the biggest sham of them all, there are so many, but "cash back" ranks right up there. Cash back is a poisoned carrot fed to first-time homebuyers, just the group who can least afford its ill effects. Under cash back, potential mortgage applicants are enticed by offers of money-back at the time of closing. This may sound tempting but there is a trade-off, a big one: *you must waive your right to negotiate an interest-rate discount on the mortgage!*

That's right, you pay the full, posted mortgage rate in exchange for the cash-back amount. It's sort of like enticing the client with his or her own money. You see, lenders are very well aware of the fact that first-time buyers are vulnerable because they are commonly short of funds at closing. It does cost additional money over and above down payment to close a house deal, and buyers are weakened when tempted with even a few hundred extra dollars. They may even ignore what could be a better deal somewhere else to get the cash-back money. They can use it to cover closing costs, or to subsidize the cost of appliances, whatever they choose. There are no rules attached to the use of the money, except that it can't form part of the down payment.

The cash-back offer draws the buyer's attention away from the real cost of the mortgage and away from any idea of negotiating a better rate. Were the cash-back money to be converted into a rate, that rate might not even be as good as the one the buyer could have easily obtained down the street at a different financial institution! No matter, the illusory effects of cash back bring blindness and deafness to what is already available in the mortgage market.

I am going to illustrate my point with a side-by-side comparison of a cash-back deal at posted rate versus a mortgage taken at a discounted rate with the discount applied, towards reduced amortization. (I will explain applying rate discounts to reduced amortization later in this chapter.) Here we have a mid-range example of a 2 percent cash back for a five-year term versus a rate discount of 75 basis points (bps) or 3/4 of 1 percent, applied to reduced amortization instead of reduced payment. For comparison purposes, we have assumed the mortgages are fully amortized.

Product	Cash Back	75 BPS Discount Applied To Reduced Amortization
Mortgage	$100,000	$100,000
Term	5 Years	5 Years
Amortization	25 Years	21.54 Years
Rate	6.95%	6.20%

Payments	$697.33	$697.33
Cash Back	$2,000.00	0
5 Yr. Balance	$90,987.02	$86,897.29
10 Yr. Balance	$78,303.99	$69,116.64
15 Yr. Balance	$60,456.49	$44,987.92
20 Yr. Balance	$35,341.58	$12,244.73
25 Yr. Balance	0	0
Total Saved	$2,000.00	$28,953.14 (payments eliminated)

We can see in the cash back column that the borrower received $2,000.00 paid up front at the time of closing and took the posted rate of 6.95 percent. By contrast, the borrower who chose to negotiate a better rate rather than be tempted by cash-back, and applied that rate discount to a reduced amortization, won the day. This borrower decided to *pay* the mortgage at the same rate as the first borrower, in other words pay $697.33 per month against an interest rate of 6.2 percent, and reduce the amortization to 21.5 years. The savings in the first five years alone is $4,089.73 but over the life of the mortgage is $697.33 x 41.52 (months saved) or $28,953.14. The bottom line is that the first borrower elected to receive $2,000 today in exchange for $28,953.14 over 25 years. The second borrower saved this large amount by maintaining the payment at $697.33 instead of opting for a reduced payment of $651.74, $45.59 per month less.

Do you now see how just $45 a month can make a world of difference? Isn't it incredible how much difference? This is another example, money management experts tell us, of how just a small amount invested over time can yield terrific returns. The difference is you are investing it in your mortgage instead of a regular investment vehicle like a savings account or a mutual fund.

Realistically, there is very little chance that the $2,000 cash-back amount could ever be invested to return $28,953.14 in 25-years' time. Besides, most people who would choose the money up-front are not likely to invest.

With just an ounce of discipline at the time the mortgage is set up, a borrower can reduce the amortization, which can be looked at as a *forced* savings plan. Once the mortgage is set up this way the borrower has *no choice* but to make the payments, reaping the benefits later on. You could argue that the borrower could not afford $45.59 a month extra. Let me tell you, if someone is entering into a $100,000 transaction and $45.59 a month is going to make or break a deal, they are getting into a home they can't afford in the first place. Besides, they would have to qualify under the higher, posted rate anyway, so they might as well take full advantage.

Can you account for $45 from your budget? (Do you have a budget?) Most people couldn't explain where $45 went in any given month. Some couldn't tell you where $500 went!

Why didn't the lender explain to the cash-back borrower what I have just explained to you? The lender didn't explain because it is his or her job to make the deal and take advantage of the advertising dollars being spent. After all, the cash-back offer is all over the radio, newspapers and various other media. He or she has a mandate to make a profit. The most profitable loan for the lender is the cash-back deal, as we have proven. It results in a full 25 years of payments at the highest rate, the posted rate for the term.

If the lender tries to be a hero and shows the cash-back client the advantage of a slightly higher payment, what would happen? The client most affected by "The E Factor" would bolt for the door like the place is on fire. He or she would search for the next lender who would be willing to give them the cash-back deal without question. Lenders, by and large, are very intelligent people. They know enough not to upset the apple cart.

Who should we blame if the lender chooses not to tell the client that $45 a month would save them $28,000 over 25 years? The lender? Partly. The bank? Partly. The client? Mostly. While we all love to do a little bank bashing from time to time, the truth here is that banks, just like most successful businesses, thrive and prosper by giving the buying public exactly what they want. They know the public will respond to cash-back offers like voters to an election promise, and so that's what the public gets!

In the final analysis, consumers must assume responsibility for the choices they make because future products and services introduced to the market will be based on those choices. I am trying to give you the knowledge to be able to make the *right* choices.

The First-Year Reduced-Payment Mortgage

In the course of your mortgage-shopping extravaganza, you might see an advertisement that reads something like this:

The 4.95 percent mortgage

You stop dead in your tracks, because the market rate for a five-year mortgage is 7.4 percent. How can this lender advertise 4.95 percent and still make money?

When you read the fine print, you find that the 4.95 percent rate is only for the first year. In the remaining four years, the rate goes back to the full, posted rate of 7.4 percent. The hook, as we must call it, is that this mortgage gives the borrower substantially reduced payments in the first year. It goes something like this. The comparisons here are for 25-year amortization and a mortgage of $100,000:

First Year Payment at 4.95%	Second Through Fifth Year at 7.4%
$578.76	$725.28

The difference is a monthly payment reduced by $146.52 for the first year. The marketing philosophy is that first-time buyers will appreciate a break in the first year while they are becoming established in their new homes. They will then be in a position to resume regular payments in the second year.

If you believe that gimmick, I've got a great deal for you on the Brooklyn Bridge! This nonsense may sound pretty good on the surface, but as you might suspect it has underlying dangers.

The people most likely to go for this sort of thing are first-time homebuyers, who are most often susceptible to "The E Factor." As well, people in this group have a tendency to incur debt after their first home purchase. They tend to forget that higher payments await, and not budget for the future. Consequently, they may incur other debts without thinking about their responsibilities, and when the deferred payments finally come due, a financial crisis emerges. It's very easy to become accustomed to a standard of living built around the lower mortgage payment.

In addition to this consideration, we need to find a way to place a value on this particular mortgage product. What is the actual value of a rate of 4.95 percent in the first year and 7.4 percent in the remaining four years? Well, without boring you with any fancy calculations, the difference is the same as if you received a rate discount of 50 bps from the posted rate of 7.4 percent or 6.9 percent. That's it. This is not very exciting, especially when you consider that a discount of 75 bps was available to the same client from the same lender! The lender has effectively used this blend of rates within a five-year term to boondoggle the client into thinking he or she just got a wonderful deal!

Just imagine. Armed with this knowledge, you find yourself in a banker's office one day and the banker places a pamphlet in front of you that describes the virtues of "The 4.95 percent Mortgage." You look it over for a few moments, perform a quick computation on your calculator you brought and say, This is equal to 50 basis points off. The average market discount is 75 basis points and up to 1 percent in some cases. Are you trying to insult my intelligence or something?

Well, they would probably have to call the paramedics because the banker would be passed out on the floor. He or she would never expect that kind of educated response from a client and that is why they can and do get away with virtually any ridiculous scheme that comes down the pike.

Once again, we have studied a mortgage gimmick that draws the attention of the borrower away from the actual cost of the product, reducing or eliminating the chances a real cost-reducing negotiation will ever take place.

The Variable Rate Mortgage

I received a rather frantic telephone call from a client one day. It went something like this:

The Story of Heather

"Hi, Mr. Baughman?"

"Yes!"

"This is Heather Brown speaking."

"Hello, Heather, how is the house hunting going?" I had acquired a pre-approval for Heather at a really attractive rate, which was then 5.95 percent or 1 percent off the then market rates, a very rare thing indeed. But Heather was an excellent credit risk so she deserved only the best.

"Well, it's going fine but the reason I called is to tell you I have found a better deal on a mortgage."

This was a surprise for me because I was sure I had secured the lowest market rate for Heather.

"What is the deal, Heather, if you don't mind me asking?"

"It's 5.5 percent for 5 years. ABC Bank is having a promotion. My friend got her mortgage there and she told me about it."

"Just a minute, Heather. There has to be a mistake somewhere. This sounds a little like a variable rate mortgage promotion to me."

"A variable rate mortgage? What's that?"

"It's a mortgage in which the rate fluctuates with the prime rate. It could be expressed as prime + 1/2 percent. Each month the mortgage rate is adjusted with the fluctuation of prime. The rate could go down and it could also go up. The bottom line is the rate is not fixed for the five-year term and you have little guarantee your payments will not increase if a substantial increase in rates comes along."

"So how can they advertise 5.5 percent for five years if it's not true?"

"It isn't 5.5 percent for five years, Heather. I can assure you if it's a variable rate mortgage the rate will be in really big print but the fine print will say this rate is only guaranteed for three months. After that it will be a certain percentage above prime for the duration of the five-year term. Some lenders even advertise below prime for a certain introductory period. Then they introduce you to the real rate."

"That's false advertising."

"No, Heather. It may be a bit deceptive, but it is not false. Legally, as long as all the true factors are disclosed, it's up to the consumer to tell the difference."

"Why do they do that? It's misleading people!"

"They do it because they know people are attracted to very low rates and so they make it look like a money sale. Like a door crasher, you know? They lure you in the door and then they have the opportunity to get your business. If after explaining the deal you don't like it, they have the opportunity to sell you something else because you are in their office and that is the most desirable place for you to be. For them, that is."

"That's awful. But wouldn't I be able to get a better deal at this same bank because they are offering such a good deal on the variable rate mortgage?"

"Not necessarily, Heather. The fact is, most often you will find a lender advertising a sweetheart deal on one mortgage product while the rest of their lineup is not attractively priced at all. People who make that assumption often end up paying more, in some cases substantially more."

"Well, I do want to know that my payments won't go up. After all, I don't think I could afford that."

"I believe you're right. Your budget is fine but if you want to remain comfortable and have money to invest, it may be the wiser choice to stay with a fixed rate mortgage like the one we have pre-approved for you. After all, we appear to be at the bottom end of a thirty-year rate cycle. I suppose it's possible for rates to go lower but it would not seem likely. Right now I think you're better off taking the longer view."

"So how will I know if ABC is really advertising a variable rate mortgage?"

"I will research it for you and call you back, how's that?"

"Great. I'll look forward to hearing from you. Have a good day!

"You too, Heather!"

I did the research for Heather as promised and it did turn out ABC Bank was promoting a variable rate mortgage. After hearing the facts, Heather decided to stay with the fixed rate five-year at 5.95 percent. With the guaranteed rate she was better able to plan her financial future, and enter into fixed-payment investing in mutual funds without having to worry about an increase in her mortgage payments upsetting that plan.

Incidentally, Heather's friend had taken the variable rate deal without understanding it fully. When Heather explained it to her she became worried about it and decided to lock in to a fixed rate, but she did so at a higher rate than she could have negotiated somewhere else. A harsh lesson.

I hope this case study has shown you how variable rate mortgages are often marketed by lenders. Here are a few important points about variable rate mortgages (VRMs).

• **VRMs are often promoted with an artificially low interest rate for a short period to attract attention, taking full advantage of "The E Factor."**

• **The payments are usually set higher than the rate. An example would be a 5 percent VRM being paid at a rate of 8 percent. This is done to reduce the balance more quickly as a hedge against the possibility of rates rising rapidly. It better prepares the bank and the borrower for the unfortunate scenario where the interest rate would exceed the rate of payment and the mortgage would begin to negatively amortize (the balance would increase with every payment made). The lenders will always take steps to prevent this before it happens, however, by increasing the borrower's monthly payment. They are obliged to do this to protect their security position.**

• **Because of the fluctuating nature of VRMs, borrowers can lose track of the actual cost of borrowing. Remember, lenders love VRMs because they can pass on rate increases to consumers immediately. If you are not careful, escalating rates in a given term can eat into monthly payments, reducing principal paid. This will retard the rate at which your balance declines and increase profits for the lender.**

• **If you become uncomfortable with the rate situation on a VRM you can, in most cases, lock in to a fixed rate mortgage without penalty, although a small fee may be required. There could, however, be a hidden penalty. We know that most borrowers who lock in do so after one or two increases in the rates have taken place. They lose their courage. That places the institution in the power position. Consequently, negotiations for a rate discount on the fixed product rarely take place, and the borrower** often pays the full, posted rate for whatever term they select. Borrowers can often end up paying up to 1 percent more for the fixed product than they would have paid had they opted for it in the first place.

• If you get angry and want to switch your mortgage elsewhere, thinking it is open, think again. Even though under the VRM you can pre-pay without penalty, you signed a contract for a five-year term. Be prepared in some cases for a whopping exit penalty!

• VRMs can be a good thing when rates are high but are on a downward trend. Borrowers can choose to go with a VRM and watch rates slide down. When they believe the bottom end has been reached, they can pay a small fee or no fee at all, and lock in to a fixed rate, while reducing their amortization.

• Smart borrowers who do this will seize the opportunity to discuss a discount on the fixed rate product. Since the pressure of an increasing-rate market is not on them, borrowers negotiate from a position of strength, and tend to use their power as customers that the bank would like to retain. Consequently, they will sometimes win a discount. However, the likelihood is that the discount will not be substantial, as the lender uses the possibility of a penalty for leaving as leverage.

• Any venture into a VRM is a gamble against the market. Be sure you can afford the gamble.

• The bank may only agree to lend you 70 percent of the value of your property on a VRM, versus 75 percent for a conventional mortgage. They reduce it because they are well aware of the volatility and the risk.

• If a VRM is going to cause you sleepless nights, don't opt for it. Life is too short and most people have better things to worry about than what the Bank of Canada or the U.S. Federal Reserve Board are going to do on any given day.

Heard about enough on variable rate mortgages? I think we have about exhausted this topic, but a lot of information was needed because VRMs are so complex.

The Rate Game

I will begin this section with a statement I've made many times in recent years: *"People are too rate conscious."*

This may sound preposterous to you. How could anyone shopping for a mortgage be too rate conscious? After all, the rate is the price paid for the mortgage, isn't it?

The fact is that the rate is only one component of the cost of a mortgage. In the chapter on debt, we saw how the total interest paid on a credit card at 12 percent exceeded that of a personal loan at 33 percent on the same amount of money. The major difference was the *time* it took the borrower to repay the credit card. So time *is* a factor, and it can have a greater effect on the overall cost of borrowing than the rate of interest itself.

Every day, people who shop the mortgage market, and perhaps even manage to stay away from the gimmicks, look to the interest rate only in determining the cost of borrowing, because that is the only way of mortgage shopping they know. Sometimes the search is so frenzied that it seems they would kill for even 5 basis points (5/100 of 1 percent). I have seen consumers do some of the strangest things for a small perceived benefit.

Part of the reason that this is so is because the cost of mortgages is advertised in terms of rate. This is how they are compared. Just look in the newspaper or your weekly real-estate guide. Look at the board in your local bank branch. The cost of mortgages is usually only expressed in terms of rate. The rate is what people concentrate on, and they do so to such a degree that they completely ignore other factors that affect the cost of borrowing, such as time and other factors we will discuss later in this chapter.

It might be helpful to compare shopping for a mortgage to shopping for a computer. Both mortgages and computers have components. Let's say you are shopping for a computer and you see the following:

Pentium Computer	Pentium Computer
$2,500	$2,200

Which one would you buy? To the untrained eye, the $2,200 computer looks like the better deal and the obvious choice. After all, a Pentium is a Pentium, right? Wrong! To someone knowledgeable in computers there is much more information required before they can make a decision. The trained person knows the aforementioned advertisements do not contain the whole story. Let's look at this again, only with more facts:

Pentium Computer
$2,500
266 MHz processor
4.0 gig hard drive
32 Mb RAM
56K fax modem

Pentium Computer
$2,200
133 MHz processor
2.0 gig hard drive
16 Mb RAM
28K fax modem

Now we see the picture! The first computer for $2,500, while a Pentium just like the other one, is far superior and a better buy since it runs at twice the speed for only $300 more. In fact, the cost of the difference in components in the first computer is much greater than $300 so it makes sense to buy the $2,500 machine. Dollar for dollar it represents a much better value.

The person who bought the $2,200 machine based on price only had an obsolete computer right out of the box. It ran just a few programs and it did so very slowly. They had not been able to see the extra *value* in paying the extra $300 instead of being fooled by the lower price. Now this person will be forced to spend additional money to upgrade and the cost will be far greater than the cost of purchasing the $2,500 machine in the first place.

Much the same kind of comparison can be made with mortgages. Let's look at a similar illustration:

5-Year-Term Mortgages
6.95 percent

5-Year-Term Mortgages
6.75 percent

I can tell you with certainty if rate were the only consideration, the lender with the 6.95 percent rate wouldn't have a chance of selling a mortgage. This is one reason why you do not see lenders advertising rates that are different from one another. They know most consumers look at rate only and do not recognize other factors. Most major lenders advertise the very same rates. But are their mortgages the same? Is a mortgage a mortgage? Let's develop this comparison more fully.

5-Year-Term Mortgages	5-Year-Term Mortgages
6.95 percent	6.75 percent
prepay up to 20 percent/year	prepay up to 10 percent/year
accelerated bi-weekly payments	bi-weekly payments
portable & assumable	portable & assumable
increase payments up to 10 percent/year	-
flexible double up payments	-
early renewals	-
no monthly fees	-
rate compounded semi-annually	-

Believe it or not, most people in the bottom 80 percent group would be so taken in by the 6.75 percent rate that they would grab it without even looking at the rest of the factors. In fact, in the case of mortgages, the other factors are not often advertised out front like they are with other products. You may have to go looking for them, just like reaching farther into the food tray to get at the more nutritious food. You may reach, only to find that they don't even exist. Lenders tend to talk only about the positive aspects of their products, and fall silent about the rest. It is up to you to know the questions to ask, and what to look for, to arrive at the true cost of borrowing.

In the above comparison you see a better rate at 6.75 percent, but a suspicious lack of information after that. Upon further investigation, you find the 6.75 percent mortgage is inferior to the 6.95 percent mortgage in the following ways:

- **Annual prepayment of only 10 percent.**
- **The bi-weekly payments are non-accelerated.**
- **No option for annual increase in monthly payments.**
- **No flexible double up payments allowed.**
- **Early renewals are not allowed.**
- **There is a service charge of $85 for scheduled renewals.**
- **The interest is compounded monthly.**

Please don't worry if you don't understand all these terms yet—we are going to discuss each of them in the next chapter so that you have a reasonable understanding on how they affect the cost of borrowing. Without putting you to sleep with a bunch of mathematical formulas, I can tell you that the 6.95 percent may well represent the better deal and result in a substantially lower cost of borrowing than the 6.75 percent mortgage. That is, if the borrower takes advantage of its many benefits. In essence, the choice would depend on the financial needs of the individual client, his or her financial plan and spending habits, points most often overlooked when selecting a mortgage.

-9-

How to Determine the True Cost of Borrowing

"Do not be made a beggar by banqueting upon borrowing, when thou hast nothing in thy purse: for thou shalt lie in wait for thine own life, and be talked on."　　　　*— Apocrypha, Ecclesiasticus 18:33.*

Before we can intelligently discuss the cost of borrowing we need a definition: The cost of borrowing is the total dollar value of all the interest charged from the day you borrow the money until the day you make the final payment.

Most people believe the cost of borrowing and rate of interest are the same thing. They are not. As we have seen, the cost of borrowing can be influenced quite substantially by factors other than rate. The cost of borrowing is the only true measure of the cost of a loan or mortgage. Let's look at its components individually.

APR (Annual Percentage Rate) Compounding

Not all rates are necessarily equal even if they look like they are. This is because of *compounding*. The more frequent the compounding the more costly the mortgage. (This is the reverse for investments, where more frequent compounding is a benefit to the consumer.) Consumers often overlook the compounding because the lender doesn't advertise it, appearing only in the fine print, which is often not read. Let's look at an example of two mortgages of the same amount, with the same rate, but different compounding.

Factor	Mortgage # 1	Mortgage #2
Mortgage Amount	$100,000.00	$100,000.00
Interest Rate	7%	7%
Compounding	semi-annually	monthly
Amortization	25 years	25 years
Monthly Payments	$700.42	$706.78
Total Payments	$210,126.00	$212,034.00
Cost of Borrowing	$110,126.00	$112,034.00
Difference		+ $1,908.00

In this example, the monthly compounding cost the second borrower $1,908 more over the life of the mortgage than the first borrower.

In Canada, most fixed rate mortgages have rates compounded semi-annually, not in advance. However, monthly compounding is common on variable rate mortgages, a fact many people miss. In addition, some credit unions use monthly compounding on all their mortgages, including fixed rate. Consumers often approach credit unions believing they automatically charge less. This is a falsehood. The fact is they very often charge more. Once again, image advertising is at work.

Amortization

Amortization is undoubtedly the one factor with the greatest impact on the cost of borrowing. Yet, consumers traditionally amortize their mortgages over 25 years, almost automatically. A five-year term and a 25-year amortization go together as naturally as a burger and fries. If you ask your lender for a quote on the monthly payment for $100,000 at 7 percent you will probably receive the answer based on a 25-year amortization. Everybody does it, don't they? Would it surprise you if I told you the bottom 80 percent do and the top 20 percent tend to opt for reduced amortization? The people who are on the fast track toward a comfortable retirement look for ways to reduce amortization because they know the tremendous impact it has on the cost of borrowing.

The reason most people shy away from a reduced amortization is because reducing amortization means increasing monthly payments. Consumers tend to think that higher payments mean the cost of borrowing is higher. The exact opposite of that is true. Higher payments will *reduce* the cost of borrowing. They are an investment in your future. The more susceptible a person is to "The E Factor," the more they will tend to avoid higher payments. They have a tendency to want to delay the inevitable by making the lowest possible payment, which often means they will make that payment for the longest possible time, with higher borrowing costs in the long run. Further, the amount they save in payments will likely be spent on things they do not need, and be eaten up with consumer debt payments.

The fact is you don't have to increase monthly payments very much to generate a significant reduction in amortization and cost of borrowing. It is truly amazing to see the differences just a few extra dollars a month can make. And so we can say, *the more you pay the less you pay*.

To illustrate, let's look at the story of two lifelong friends who negotiated their mortgages at the same time, many years ago.

The Story of John and Fred

John and Fred both went out shopping for a $100,000 mortgage. John did much better, or so it would seem, grinding his banker to tears and winning a 5.95 percent mortgage, 1 percent below the posted rate at 6.95 percent. Fred was not as skilled a negotiator and he had a grumpy banker. He wound up with only a 1/2 percentage point off, a 6.45 percent. Although Fred would pay a higher rate, he had a plan. (The comparison below assumes that both mortgages are fully amortized over twenty-five years).

Item	John	Fred
Mortgage	$100,000.00	$100,000.00
Term	5 Years	5 Years
Amortization	25 Years	22.5 Years
Rate	5.95%	6.45%
Payments	$636.84	$697.33

Total Repaid	$191,052.00	$188,279.00
Difference		$2,773.00
Value of Mortgage Payments Eliminated		$19,000.00

Even though Fred paid a higher rate, he was finished paying 2.5 years *earlier* than John and saved over $19,000! How?

- **Fred decided to take his smaller rate discount in the form of a reduced amortization. His payments were set at the amount they would have been had he paid the full posted rate of 6.95 percent, a difference of $60.49 per month.**
- **John, having conquered his banker for 1 percent off, took the lower payment. He wound up paying more in borrowing costs than his friend. He never really knew where the $60.49 went that he "saved" each month. It just disappeared.**
- **At the end of 22.5 years, Fred decided to continue making the mortgage payments of $697.33. After all, they had become a habit. The difference was he paid them to himself, towards an investment with an average rate of return of 8 percent per annum, compounded annually. At the end of the 25 years he had saved approximately $22,900 in total!**

John still tells the story of how he won the big discount from his banker. And Fred just smiles. A low rate is fine. But it's what you do with it that counts. *The more you pay — the less you pay!*

This story demonstrates how far off-the-mark people are in thinking of the price of a mortgage only in terms of rate. Yet, this way of thinking permeates our society.

Just because you have won a sizeable discount in mortgage rate, does not mean you have won the day. Unless that discount is used the right way, you will gain very little benefit from it. The right way is to apply the discount to a reduced amortization.

Frequency of Payment

Most lending institutions offer the standard payment frequencies, with weekly and bi-weekly being the most popular. What many people fail to realize is that these come in two forms, accelerated and non-accelerated. What's the difference? Lets look at the following illustration:

Accelerated Bi-Weekly Payment
$350.21

Bi-Weekly Payment
$323.27

You may be surprised to learn that these two payments are for the same mortgage: $100,000 at 7 percent over 25 years. The monthly payment is $700.42.

How do we arrive at the payments? For accelerated, it's just the monthly payment divided by two. For non-accelerated, it's the monthly payment x 12/26. The term "accelerated" means the balance will be repaid faster, indicated by the higher payment amount. With accelerated bi-weekly, you are effectively paying one full additional payment each year (broken down into 26 parts).

Here's the amortization of two mortgages, both bearing the same rate and amount, but with different types of bi-weekly payments:

Factor	Mortgage #1 Accelerated	Mortgage # 2 Non- Accelerated
Mortgage Amount	$100,000.00	$100,000.00
Rate of Interest	7% APR semi-annual	7% APR semi-annual
Bi-Weekly Payment	$350.21	$323.27
Total Payments	$187,015.64	$209,262.37
Cost of Borrowing	$87,015.64	$109,262.37
Difference		+ $22,246.73
Repaid In	534.01 payments (20.54 years)	647.33 payments (24.90 years)

As you can see, there is a staggering difference in the cost of borrowing between the two different types of bi-weekly payments, and here is where some people lose out. Lenders will sometimes not say up front what type of bi-weekly payment you are getting, and since most consumers do not know how to tell the difference, they may be paying significantly higher borrowing costs without knowing it. They may in fact not realize it until years down the road, when they see that the mortgage balance is much higher than they expected it to be.

There was a trust company, now out of business, which used to advertise the many good features of its mortgage products, and they *were* very good. However, this company failed to inform people that their bi-weekly payments were non-accelerated. Consequently, because the lender makes more money on non-accelerated bi-weekly payments, this was their way of helping to pay for the other perks they gave out. Give and take, if you will. Or perhaps, bait and switch?

You can see that the non-accelerated does reduce the amortization - by little more than a month. If a lender is asked if the bi-weekly payments reduce amortization, he can answer in the affirmative. Do you see why we need strict consumer laws on the disclosure of the true cost of borrowing? The current laws do not go far enough.

Prepayment Privileges

Prepayment privileges on closed, fixed rate mortgages can come in many forms. The term "closed" means the lender is under no obligation to allow you to pay even a dollar more per month than the agreed-upon amount. Sometimes lenders will allow prepayment, but charge a three-month interest penalty on the amount prepaid. In other cases they will allow certain pre-defined privileges:

Flexible Double up Payments
Though there are differing rules, this one allows you to pay up to twice the monthly payment in any given month. In most cases, you don't have to make a full double payment which most people can't afford–you can pay as little as $100, but not more than double.

Anniversary Lump Sum Payment
On the anniversary of your mortgage, you can pay a fixed percentage of the balance as allowed by the lender. This percentage can range from 10 percent to 20 percent. Some lenders want the pay-

ment on the anniversary date; if you miss it you have to wait until the following year. Other lenders will allow the anniversary to float; you can pay the lump sum anytime during the calendar year.

Annual Payment Increase

Some lenders will allow you to increase your monthly payments by a fixed percentage, most commonly 10 percent, but some by as much as 20 percent. For example, your payment could start out at $700.42 in the first year, and be increased in the second year to $770.46, in the third year to $847.51, etc.

These are the most common kinds of prepayment privileges. They vary from lender to lender, so it is crucial that you ask specific questions to root out the facts.

We have already established that increased payment reduces amortization and can have a significant downward influence on borrowing costs. If you take advantage of the prepayment privileges as best you can, you will be debt free years sooner.

The problem is most people do not have the discipline to pay additional amounts on their mortgage. I would say only the best of the best, perhaps the top 5 percent will do so. For the rest, if you want to significantly reduce borrowing costs, it's advisable to reduce the amortization from the beginning. In this manner you will be locked in to the slightly higher payments you need to reduce interest charges.

Fees

You should resist the attempt of any lender to charge fees over and above what is being charged in the interest rate. This holds true for *renewal fees, appraisal fees, application fees and other fees*, which most lenders will waive if asked.

Monthly fees may crop up on the commitment letter or the pre-approval certificate. You have to read the fine print, as the lender may not say anything about them when you are shopping. Ask the questions. Remember, lenders don't like to talk about the negative aspects of their products.

I once found monthly fees in a commitment letter from a lender to whom I had referred a client. I called to ask about this extra charge of $3 per month. The lender tried to say it was charged in lieu of a renewal fee. But if the clients were taking a 10-year term they would pay $360 in total–a pretty hefty renewal fee. I wrote "waived" on the mortgage offer and sent it in. The lender accepted the change, something I knew would happen. The client saved $360.

The only fees you may be forced to pay are those the lender has paid, such as an application fee to a mortgage default insurer or an appraiser. However, if you negotiate, some lenders will absorb this cost as well.

Please remember that fees, while they are a nuisance, are just a small component of the overall cost of a mortgage. Fight them off, but don't lose sight of the big picture. You now know where the significant costs of a mortgage really lie–concentrate on them first and don't allow yourself to be so distracted by the small things that you miss a big one.

Portability

Portability is a very good feature. It allows a borrower to transfer the existing mortgage balance, terms and rate from one property to another. When rates have increased, portability allows you to take your lower-rate mortgage with you to the next property and borrow only the additional amount you need at today's higher rates.

In that sense, portability is definitely a component of the cost of borrowing. You can save thousands by porting a low-rate mortgage rather than borrowing all over again at higher market rates.

Here is a case study about mortgage portability which will illustrate its usefulness and teach us an important lesson.

The Story of Dave and Madeline

Dave and Madeline acquired their mortgage through a local credit union. They liked the idea of aquiring it there because they had heard that credit unions were friendlier than banks, that they just seemed to care more about their clients and treat them better. Dave and Madeline had not been satisfied with the level of service they were receiving from their current bank, so the decision to go with a credit union was an easy one.

When the mortgage was negotiated, Dave and Madeline won

approval at a rate that was 25 basis points below the best rate their bank would give them. The credit union approved a mortgage for $135,000 at 6.5 percent on a three-year term with 25-year amortization. They were extremely happy about the deal. A lower rate and better service? Who could complain about that?

At the end of the first year in their new house, Dave's boss told him that the company was in financial trouble. Dave's job was being eliminated, but he would not be out of work, as a new position was being created for him at the company's affiliate in Calgary. The company would cover moving expenses, with some exceptions. Dave had been very well aware of the possibility of a move for a few years, as it had been discussed with him on several occasions.

Dave and Madeline were very excited about moving to a new city and the opportunity for a fresh start. That is, until they visited their credit union to inquire about having their mortgage transferred or ported over to their new home in Calgary. Rates had gone up in the last year and they wanted to retain their good rate while only borrowing a small amount at the higher rate to complete the purchase.

The lender announced the credit union did not have any branches in Alberta. As a result, the mortgage could not be transferred and would have to be paid off with the sale of their home. They would incur a three-month interest penalty and the cost of discharge, a total of $2,278.41. Dave's company refused to absorb this cost so Dave and Madeline were about to suffer an erosion of their equity.

Was this the only cost Dave and Madeline would incur as a result of their mortgage not being portable to Calgary? Certainly not. Let's not forget that they signed up for a three-year term at 6.5 percent and still had two years to go. In the past year, rates had climbed to 8 percent for a three-year term. So, in addition to the penalty, they lost an interest advantage, having to borrow the full amount for the next home at the higher rate. The rate differential, expressed as a dollar value, was approximately $4,695 so the total interest penalty was in excess of $6,900.

Dave and Madeline pleaded with the credit union to waive the penalty. They had neglected to consider the portability feature when they got their mortgage, even though they knew there was a chance they would be transferred. They were so enamoured with the rate they didn't see anything else. Their arguments fell on deaf ears, as the credit union refused to give them any consideration, charging the full penalty allowable under the contract.

Dave and Madeline learned a very valuable and expensive lesson: *look beyond the rate!* Beyond the rate is where treasures lie. Beyond the rate is also where traps are set. Fail to look beyond the rate and you may well suffer the consequences.

Dave and Madeline, in choosing a credit union over their bank, effectively negotiated a 25 basis point rate discount worth just over $2,000 in exchange for a penalty of $6,900. Had they chosen to go with a bank in this case their mortgage would have been fully portable to Calgary.

As I always say, the onramp to a mortgage can be very friendly indeed, but the exit ramp can be paved with land mines! Portability is truly a serious component of the cost of borrowing, as Dave and Madeline learned. It's a fact of life today, given the unsettled work environment, that people have to be more mobile than ever. This is why portability is such an important feature for your mortgage.

There is another component to the cost of a mortgage we haven't discussed yet–early renewal. It too can also have a major impact on the cost of borrowing. We'll cover it in a later chapter in more detail. For now, let's just say that any mortgage you sign your name to should include a right to early renew. If that right isn't part of the contract, then there should be some evidence the financial institution is allowing its customers to early renew anyway.

We have come a long way. There is a great deal you need to know about mortgages if you are to shop for one effectively. I've done my best to condense the information–even so, I recognize there is a lot to absorb. I would recommend you come back to this chapter after you're finished reading this book. This information is just too important to miss as I'm sure you have learned.

Consumers need to look at the banking relationship in a whole new light. They need to know the truth about borrowing costs and how to determine them. They need to know how to decipher all of the information they receive on a daily basis from advertising. They need to know how to recognize half-truths, and to ferret out information being held back. They need to know the pertinent questions to ask, and how to ask them. A mortgage is just too important to be taken lightly, as mistakes made in setting one up can be costly. They can, in fact, upset your financial plan.

-10-

Shopping for a Mortgage

"Nowadays people know the price of everything and the value of nothing."
— *Oscar Wilde, The Picture of Dorian Gray.*

Recently, I received a call from a woman who was shopping for a mortgage, or so she thought. It seemed she really didn't know much about mortgages. Her husband had asked her to call around to various lenders to obtain quotes.

The woman wanted to know how much the monthly payments would be on a mortgage of $200,000. Apparently these people thought that the lowest payment would be the best indicator of the least costly mortgage for them.

In effect, this woman was asking me, how can I make sure that I pay for my mortgage for as long as possible, perhaps even into retirement, and how can I increase my borrowing costs well beyond what is necessary?

Several years ago, I began to take notice of and study the mortgage shopping habits of consumers. What I found was that the top 20 percent were fairly knowledgeable and would make a conscious effort to search out the best mortgage. The top 5 percent were very knowledgeable, and could be counted on to know most of what there was to know about mortgages, while securing the best deals available in the marketplace.

By contrast, the bottom 80 percent did not make any noticeable effort to shop the market. They had a tendency to drift in the direction of whatever financial institution they were currently dealing with and to take whatever deal that institution would offer. They were convinced that whatever deal their "own bank" gave them was the best deal for them.

As a result, I came to the conclusion–and I still maintain it today–that most consumers shop less for a mortgage, the largest financial contract they will likely ever sign, than they do for a pair of shoes. Day after day, in my study of mortgage shopping habits I witnessed people unknowingly assigning themselves to additional years of mortgage payments unnecessarily. I found that with very little effort they could have chopped two or three years off of their mortgage, saving tens of thousands of dollars.

I began to discuss my findings with many of my colleagues and they invariably agreed that there was a tendency among consumers to ignore the choices available to them in the mortgage market. I also came to the conclusion that most people would believe whatever advice their banker gave them, as if it were the Ten Commandments being delivered to Moses. What's more, they would tune out anyone who was offering opposing advice, even if it was the correct advice for them.

I spoke to mortgage clients and asked them questions about the process they had been through. In some cases I pointed out how mistakes could have been avoided and they would, almost always, fall back on the advice their banker had given them as the reason for the choices they made. This led to the only logical conclusion I could possibly reach: *the major reason people do not shop for mortgages is that they do not know how.*

Most people have no training whatsoever in financial planning or in dealing with financial institutions. Information they need has not been made available to them. In my research, I was stunned at the lack of information that exists on these subjects. I did my best to find it, figuring that someone must have written about it before, but to no avail. In Canada, this information did not seem to exist.

It is human nature to shy away from the unknown. The unknown incites fear, and fear can be tempered, in the case of shopping for mortgages, with the familiarity of one's "own bank." It acts almost as a safe house to shield people, who lack the education to take on the mortgage market, from the unknown.

Bankers are paid to maximize profit. By contrast, you are on a quest to get the lowest cost mortgage. You must realize that these two missions are completely at odds with each other. Is the banker dishonest? No, most bankers are very honest. Nevertheless, their mandate to make a profit is a very powerful driving force. In some cases, their jobs, their families and their own financial future depends on it. The stakes are very high indeed and this pressure sometimes results in half-truths being told, or the omission of important information that could result in years of unnecessary mortgage payments for you. So it is your mission, as well as your challenge, to educate yourself so that you can begin to filter out all the information, and separate the good advice from the bad.

A Second Opinion

I received a call one day from a young man who was buying his first home. He had been working with a real-estate-agent and was already pre-approved for a mortgage. However his instincts told him to get at least a second opinion. I arranged to meet him at his home for a consultation.

During the session, my client mentioned that he was motivated to call me because of the exchange he had with the first banker he encountered.

"There was something strange about the whole business," he said.

"What do you mean?"

"Well, the banker told me she was giving me 25 basis points off the market rate because I had decided to buy my home through ABC real-estate Company and that it was the best deal I would get."

I had been writing comments while the client was talking, and I looked up at him in surprise. As our eyes met and in total silence, I began to smile. Then he began to smile. I smiled wider. He smiled wider. We then broke out in laughter simultaneously.

"It's nonsense, isn't it?"

"Yes sir, the purest variety."

This banker had attempted to make the client believe his decision to purchase a home though a particular real-estate firm was the one factor that caused the bank to cave in to a rate discount. The reason she gave was that this branch maintained an ongoing relationship with the real-estate firm, and was promoting them in a positive light in exchange for business referred.

The banker lied. The only reason she was about to grant a rate concession was that the client qualified for it and she was forced to reduce the rate to compete. Period. In addition, the generosity of the discount was also misrepresented. At that time, the average discount available to the average borrower was 50 basis points, and higher for clients with above-average qualifications.

This client received his 50 basis points discount, which I arranged for him. What would have happened had he not decided to get a second opinion, and check the validity of the information he was receiving? Like many consumers who would have fallen for that advice, he would have paid a significantly higher price for the mortgage. The banker has a mandate to lend money at the highest possible rate, in the name of profitability, and to make the client feel wonderful about it.

Banks thrive on the loyalty of their clients. When I was a banker, it was always easier for me to deal with a loyal client because there was little danger of losing their business. It was easier because I knew I did not have to give anything away, and I could fulfill my mandate to maximize profit. I would never knowingly render the wrong advice to a client, but I would keep the perks locked away in the bottom drawer whenever the opportunity presented itself.

A good banker can sense a client's loyalty just as a shark can sense fresh blood in the water. Within the first three minutes of talking to a client, the banker knows exactly which direction the session will go and how it will turn out. He or she will probably know what rate the client will receive, how long the mortgage will be amortized and what additional services the client can be sold. The banker can do this by assessing the personality of the client, and knowing the length of dealings, which the customer mistakenly reveals, along with other things, during the course of the conversation.

Through it all, the banker will never admit to knowing the outcome. He or she will listen intently, making the client feel as comfortable as possible, while punching the terms of the deal they know the client will take into the computer. For the experienced banker, I must tell you in all honesty, this is like shooting fish in a barrel. It is so ridiculously easy it defies description. Yet, there is nothing misrepresented, no lies being told, and no half-truths. The need for any of those things is eliminated because of the degree of loyalty expressed by the consumer.

The Sting

Jack, a salesman of considerable expertise, was called upon to help his mother and father-in-law, Irene and Tom, shop for a car. They were going to drive out of town to a small community, which was really an oasis of automobile dealers, an area the general public believed offered the best deals around.

Jack fully expected that this day would be a long one. It was a Saturday, a very busy day for car dealers, and with so much to choose from, he knew it would be quite an adventure. He was going to employ his superior negotiating skills to win a sizeable saving for Irene and Tom.

As they drove into town they spotted a large General Motors dealership and decided to stop there. Jack knew Tom was a GM man, and that he would probably not be comfortable going to a Ford or Chrysler dealership first, if at all. GM had indeed won his loyalty.

They walked around the lot kicking tires for a while, about five minutes or so, and spotted a slightly experienced Chevy Caprice. They summoned a salesman, who retrieved the keys and accompanied them on a test drive.

As they drove along, Tom gave an account of his success with GM cars over the years, much to the delight of the salesman, who freely seized the opportunity to engage Tom in conversation. The salesman could sense his loyalty to GM, and he sensed Tom and Irene might be easy prey.

As they returned to the dealership, Jack could see that Irene was warming up to this car and that worried him, because if he could see it, the salesman was probably already deciding what he was going to do with his commission. Jack thought that that could really interfere with his goal, which was to help Tom and Irene get the best car at the best price. Just as they came to a stop, Irene wound up and kicked the legs right out from under Jack.

"Sold," she announced. Irene was a wonderful woman, but she was just plain out of line. Although Jack had coached her not to say anything, she could not contain her love for the car.

Jack's jaw dropped and his heart sank into the pit of his stomach. Game over. The salesman knew Irene loved the car and intended to buy it. In all likelihood, the price had just gone up! The salesman never changed his facial expression. Jack was on the floor in the back seat, but the salesman didn't even flinch. Jack was both dazed and impressed!

After Jack collected himself, they went into the salesman's office, a desk in the showroom, to take care of the paperwork. The salesman announced the price of the car and with an accommodating nod from Irene, began to write up the bill of sale. Never being one to give up, Jack bravely attempted to negotiate a better price. The salesman looked at Jack as though Jack had just arrived from outer space. He was sending a message that he knew he had Irene just where he wanted her, and that it was probably time for Jack to go get a free hot dog. Jack looked at Irene and she was sending the same message, so he did what any self-respecting super salesman would do in a situation like that: he went for a hot dog! That was about the only thing Jack was going to get for free that day.

Irene had probably cost herself $1,500. She could have saved by containing her love of the product and making the salesman work for his commission. Nevertheless, the $1,500 wasn't going to make that much difference in her financial future and besides, she walked away happy while Jack licked his wounds.

I must tell you that many people, just like Tom and Irene, walk away from their own banks every day, happy as they can be, after placing their financial future in jeopardy through a badly executed mortgage negotiation. A mortgage loan and a used car purchase, however, cannot be compared in their impact. It's no contest.

Shop where you are not known

When shopping for a mortgage, it is often best to shop where you are not known. Imagine for a moment how a banker would react upon hearing of a new client entering the branch to apply for a mortgage. Many years ago, it was more difficult to win approval for a loan if you were not known. That is ancient history. Today, if a banker learns of a new client in the branch, he or she will reach down and quietly unlock the bottom drawer where all the perks and incentives are! They do that because they know the client probably has a one-sided cozy relationship with another bank, and they will have to haul out the perks and incentives to win their business.

If you are still concerned about being known, please understand that the banker can get to know you in seconds simply by pulling up a credit report. They can see, through the wonders of technology, who you really are, for their purposes. Your credit report attests to your character, as well as your ability and intent to repay, the most significant aspects of the lending decision. So please cast aside any fears about not being known.

The reality is that good bankers will do their best to contain their glee at the opportunity to land a new customer. Deep inside, they are jumping for joy, because they know what a competitive struggle it is these days. The bank gives them a set of weekly or monthly goals, which are usually cast in stone. Bankers today often operate with guns to their heads; they must produce or they are history, and I'm not exaggerating. Good new borrowing clients are hard to come by these days, with so many people affected by the globalized economy, and with the baby boomers moving off into their investment years.

The good banker really wants your new business, and will bid for it, but you must never lose sight of the fact that profit is still the central mandate. They must win the new business and make it profitable too, so you must be on your guard while being welcomed with open arms. Can you do it? I'm sure you can!

The Sales Initiative

You may say you don't like sales, but most people, whether they want to admit it or not, are in sales. If you have a job, on a daily basis you are engaged in selling your employer on the idea of keeping you or letting you go through your performance. In this case, you are selling a product to a lender. It is your job to convince the lender to buy the product at the most attractive price for you. It is the lender's job to offer buyer resistance and go against your price objective. The degree of success you have depends on your selling skills and the quality of product you are selling.

And just exactly what are you selling? You are selling you. That's right. By making a decision to grant a mortgage the lender is really making an investment in you. You are in every sense the product. In fact, the lender is really just an intermediary in the transaction, acting for an investor whose money will ultimately be used to fund your mortgage. It's the lender's job, as we discussed earlier, to act in the best interests of the investor by making sure any investments made are well justified. The investors expect only the best performance from the lenders, and losses through bad judgement are just not tolerated.

I want you to imagine that you are going to a sales meeting with a prospective client (the lender) to negotiate a $100,000 contract (your mortgage). The stakes are very high. It's perhaps the biggest deal of your life. There can be no foul-ups. Can you imagine how you would prepare for the biggest sales initiative of your lifetime?

Think about it for a moment. I've already prepared you with a good overall knowledge of the mortgage product, and certainly you have at least a fair idea about pricing. You also know how to deflect the mortgage gimmicks that are going to be flung at you. But is there anything else? Here are a few points for consideration.

Dress Appropriately

Dress for success, they say. It's true and not only in banking. You are going to a business meeting, perhaps the most important one of your life. I'm not suggesting you go out and rent formal wear, just dress sensibly–no jeans or cut offs. A suit would be nice, but even a good pair of slacks and a clean shirt and shoes are fine for men. For the women, I probably don't have to say. You'll already have the idea.

Leave Your Children at Home! I've wanted to say this for years!

Would you take your kids to a major business meeting? I'm sure the prospect would be quite unimpressed. I'm also sure it would be a very short meeting.

People do bring their kids and for the most part it drives bankers crazy. Children distract both the banker and the mortgage applicant, not something I recommend with $100,000 on the line. Plan ahead and get a baby-sitter if you have to. Your attention has to be fully focused on the sales initiative.

Carry a Legal Size Sales Folder, Preferably in a Briefcase

Lenders hate it when people are unprepared. That's why your folder should contain a wealth of information about you, and everything the lender needs in order to make a decision and issue you a pre-approval right on the spot. None of this we'll-call-you-in-two-or-three-days business. I'm going to give you a list so that you will be armed to the teeth with information, and capable of fielding most every question the lender might have.

Remember to make enough copies so that each lender you visit can have one. If you are going to shop three lenders, take three complete folders. Here's what each folder should contain:

Credit Report

• You should have a copy of your credit report, which you have already studied yourself to make sure all the information is accurate.
• Any mistakes should have already been addressed with the credit bureau.
• You should have detailed and credible explanations ready for any incidence of late payment or otherwise unsatisfactory credit history.

Employment Verification Letter

You should have a letter from your employer stating the following:
• date started
• position or occupation
• salary or commission arrangement
• status–whether full-time, part-time or seasonal
• hourly rate, if applicable, together with number of hours in a regular work week
• overtime should be itemized separately
• whether or not you are on probation

T4s and Pay Stubs

• Lenders will sometimes ask for T4s and pay stubs as additional support for proof of income–best have them ready.
• Your most recent pay stub should suffice.
• T4s should go back three years or as far back as you can.

Financial Statements

If you are self employed:
• You will need financial statements for the last three full years of operations and Revenue Canada notices of assessment going back three years.
• Lenders will take a dim view if your statements are not up to date. They look at it as a sign that the business is not well run. Don't apply until your statements are in order.

• Your Revenue Canada notices of assessment will be used to verify that your returns have been filed, and that you pay your taxes without arrears. Once again, it's best to clean up any tax arrears before you apply, because tax arrears are a signal that the business is in negative cash flow.

Proof of Down Payment

If you're buying a home you will need a down payment, and proof that you have the funds to cover it. Therefore, you should bring:

• Bank statements for the last three months showing an accumulation of savings from any of the accounts on which you intend to draw the down payment.

• Copies of any mutual fund statements and/or certificates of deposit from which the down payment will be taken.

• If all or a part of your down payment is a gift from a relative the lender will provide you with a gift-letter form to be completed. When filled out, it will declare that the gifter is giving you a specified amount, which does not have to be repaid.

Credit Information

Your credit report will contain most of your credit information. However, since there are still some members who do not regularly report to the bureau, it may be advisable to bring your loan or mortgage statements along with the most recent credit card statements.

Asset Information

Bring a listing of all your assets including cash, property and vehicles, together with their approximated values.

Identification

I shouldn't have to mention this, but people do show up at the bank without their identification. The bank will need your identification, and will want to record your social insurance number. (There is nothing sinister behind the bank's request for your social insurance number. They use it to positively identify you from other bank clients and they need it to access accurate credit information. If they can't get the credit information because you have refused to provide the number then the decision will go against you. There's no spy stuff. Give them your social insurance number.)

Know Your Affordability Threshold

You should, after performing your own affordability test, know *exactly* how much you can afford to pay each month on a mortgage. If the lender says you can afford more, just explain that you are comfortable with the amount you calculated. Please do not be tempted to indulge yourself beyond that point.

Where's The Lender's Bottom Line?

It helps to let the lender know you are cognizant of the market rates and what discounts are available. Discounted mortgage rates are often advertised in real-estate publications by lenders and mortgage brokers alike. Your realtor is bombarded with mortgage information on a daily basis and this information is yours for the asking. That's why it's not very difficult these days to find out where a lender's true bottom line is.

Remember, however, advertisements do not show the bottom line. Thus, it is a general rule of thumb that the real bottom line is usually somewhere from 25 to 50 basis points below the best rate you can find in print. If you see advertising showing a maximum 75 bps discount, you can be fairly sure that 100 or even 125 bps are available. You have to be good to get the back-room rate – they don't give it away like candy. After all, you must remember the lender is in business to make a profit. Nevertheless, considering your current state of readiness, you are already on your way towards a sizeable saving.

The degree to which you prepare for any sales presentation or negotiation, together with the quality of delivery of that presentation and the quality of your product are the key factors that will determine your success. It won't make any difference that you have dealt with the bank for twenty years. It won't make any difference your family has embraced the bank for generations. No, it won't even make a difference if you have the bank's logo tattooed on your forehead. Concentrate on what you now know to be the key factors and you will be more successful.

If you show up dressed for business and ready to do business you will be in the top 10 or 20 percent of mortgage applicants because the rest just don't get it. I can tell you with certainty that preparation will pay off for you in making a positive impression on the lender and it could perhaps mean the difference between denial and approval if your application is marginal. The entire negotiation should go more smoothly and yield a better result.

How to establish the qualifications of your lender

As you meet your lender, and after you have engaged in a few moments of small talk, it will be advisable to state the purpose of your visit and get right down to business. *At this time you should establish the qualifications of your lender!*

Most people are so intimidated by their bankers that they wouldn't dream of asking them for a résumé or an outline of their qualifications for mortgage lending. Yet, this is a major mistake for most mortgage applicants, and it can, and often does, mean the difference between success and failure.

The experience level of your lender does matter, just like the experience of your doctor matters. I can count on one hand the number of times I was asked over the years about my level of experience. The clients who did ask impressed me every time.

Remember when we discussed name-brand loyalty, and interviewing a new branch manager? We concluded that among bankers there were power abusers and those who enjoyed using their power to do good things and achieve outstanding results for their clients as well as for the financial institution. Win-win, right? Well, anyone who would be offended by a question about qualifications to handle your $100,000 transaction can be readily identified as an abuser, and you should terminate that interview immediately!

Your current state of readiness for this meeting is already enough to neutralize much of the power any banker will hold over you. This is a step towards levelling out the playing field. Then, if you ask for qualifications, that levels it out even more.

The positive banker may not have a résumé in their bottom drawer ready for your inspection, but they will be very happy to give you an outline of their experience orally.

The negative banker will give you a reaction that tells you right away you have crossed the line. He or she will act threatened and perhaps even angry. That is your signal it may be time to go to the next meeting. Negative-power bankers are troublemakers who spend much of their time playing political games so common within the "hallowed halls" of the financial institution. You do not want to know them.

In establishing the experience level of your lender, it is absolutely vital that you determine where their comfort zone lies. You see, it used to be that a lender engaged only in the practice of lending. If you wanted to talk about mutual funds, the lender would refer you to someone experienced in that field. However, in the 1990s, expense reduction and consolidation led to the banks deciding that it was necessary to have one person do both jobs. Enter the financial advisor.

The Financial Advisor

The Financial Advisor is the title often given to this new type of bank employee. They perform lending duties, as well as sell mutual funds and other investment products. It has been my experience, however, that people are not comfortable doing both things. One person may have a comfort zone in lending, the other in investment banking. Apparently, a small percentage of bankers are just as good at lending as they are selling. Personally, though, I have never met one of these people.

The comfort zone is important because people perform at their best within their own comfort zone. So, you would be much better off to pick what I would call a purebred lender if you're looking for a mortgage and a purebred financial advisor if you want investment advice. It just makes sense.

Pose a non-threatening question like, "What do you enjoy most about your job, lending or selling mutual funds?" The banker, if a positive-power banker, will answer truthfully and will display a genuine interest in their comfort zone field.

If you determine your lender is really a career financial advisor who is in his first week in lending you should politely ask to see someone experienced in mortgage lending. This practice is not offensive. You have every right to choose a lender you'll have confidence in. After all, we are talking about your $100,000 here, aren't we?

There is an element of the ridiculous in all of this. I wrote this book to try to help you prepare for the largest financial negotiation of your life. We are both investing our time and working hard to make it a success. At the same time, it is entirely possible the financial institution places nowhere near the same degree of importance we do on this meeting and will gladly send someone who is ill-prepared to represent it. Who is the richer? Life is very perverse, in a way.

I have had some interesting experiences with bank employees trying to do jobs they weren't right for. Some financial institutions are understandably having trouble with this new, consolidated position. A bank in one city had a team of financial advisors who were all from investment-banking backgrounds. They were asked to serve mortgage clients and just fumble through it as best they could. If they ran into trouble they could call a "mortgage expert" downtown to "talk them through it." Apparently, the bank thought it was more cost efficient to have one person, knowledgeable in mortgages, at a central location, than to have experienced lenders in every branch. Would you want to be represented by a banker who had to be "talked through" your transaction? Very scary!

Bottom line, if you say the word "mortgage" to your financial advisor and he turns as pale as a ghost, his eyes roll back and he passes out on the floor, get out of there like you would a burning house, okay?

Assuming that you have found a competent and positive-power purebred lender, (the only kind to have), the application process should go smoothly, merely an exchange of information between you and the banker.

At this point, with all of the documentation you have brought, the lender should be able to make a decision as to your qualification for the mortgage right on the spot. Please remember there's no need for the lender to pull another credit report. You gave them a copy. Explain to the lender that you are aware of the negative effect inquiries have on your credit score. If they still insist, it is up to you to decide what action to take. A really good, competent lender, in order to protect the bank's interests, will set a condition that a report be pulled for the bank's own purposes before final approval is granted. That's okay. It is, however, your judgement call.

Now that you have the lender interested in your business, having seen the quality of your product, it's time to proceed from the sales initiative to pricing. There is a step in between we can't miss, though.

Term Selection

Invariably, people would ask me for advice on which term to take. They wanted to know where the interest rates were going. Dear reader, if I knew that I wouldn't have been working for a bank! I would be out looking for the next exotic beach, a millionaire many times over.

Many consumers make the mistake of relying on advice from the banker, which is often biased towards a certain result (I'll elaborate later). But the basic error consumers make is that they look at term selection as a means of hedging their bets against what the mortgage market will do. If the rates are going up they want a longer term. If the rates are going down they want a shorter term. The problem is that nobody really knows where the rates are going, so it only makes sense to base your decision on more reliable data. Does that make sense to you? I hope so.

It's practically impossible for me to outline all of the factors that should go into term selection because the primary consideration should be the financial condition of the applicant and his or her overall financial plan. Since many in the bottom 80 percent group don't even have a financial plan, they fall victim to playing the market and they often lose substantially. (With all due respect, if you want to gamble against the market, buy some stocks and use risk capital only. Don't gamble with your house! There are many more losers than winners.) These people are looking to get the lowest possible payment and they don't care if it takes three hundred years to pay off their mortgage. As a matter of fact they probably don't even think about that.

Short-Term Theories

There are some truly ridiculous theories in the marketplace about term selection, and the most common are the short-term theories. The short-term theories say that you will always be on the bottom end of the rate scale if you take the shortest term. Therefore, the lower payment yielded by the lowest rate is the answer for everyone. These theories rely on reduced payment as the vehicle to reduced borrowing costs, and they ignore amortization.

In fact, short-term theories can really get someone into trouble! It is amazing that given that we are at the bottom end of a thirty-year rate cycle, as this book is being written, people would still be talking about short-term rates.

There was a study released recently by a major bank that put forward the theory that 1-year terms yielded the best results. The best results for whom? This was simply a rate-study that took only payment savings into consideration not amortization. In addition, the study implied that this theory would work for everyone, ignoring the financial needs of individual borrowers. It was pure nonsense.

Here is a story about a couple who embraced this theory.

The story of Bill and Sharon

I once visited this nice couple at their home. They wanted to refinance their mortgage – that's all they told me when they called. When I arrived, Bill poured coffee, and we waited for Sharon who was late, tied up in traffic.

During our wait, Bill and I engaged in general conversation about mortgages. He immediately started talking about the old short-term theories. Bill was sold on always going short term, and benefiting from being at the bottom end of the rate scale. He claimed it saved him at least $150 per month. No telling what the savings could amount to over the life of the mortgage.

I started to tell Bill that I thought it best to look at an individual's overall financial situation and financial plan before deciding on the term. He immediately cut me off, saying I was wrong. Short term was trendy. He got the idea from a friend (the kiss of death) who had also saved money, and that was that. There was no way he was going to listen to any other theory.

Since I could see Bill was very opinionated, I was looking for a way to change the subject. Just then, Sharon walked in and we sat down to what I now thought could be a very challenging session.

Bill and Sharon told me that they wanted to consider re-mortgaging their home so that they could consolidate a few debts. Here is an outline of Bill and Sharon's debts as I listed them that day:

Creditor Payments	Limit	Balance	Monthly
Car Loan		$9,945	$343
Credit Card	$3,000	$1,900	$95
Credit Card	$9,000	$7,215	$360

Credit Card	$6,000	$5,500	$275
Credit Card	$7,000	$7,000	$350
Credit Card	$4,500	$2,212	$110
Line of Credit	$20,000	$18,000	$540
Loan		$11,500	$510
Auto Lease			$589
Property Taxes		$2,000	
Mortgage		$61,000	$450
Totals	$49,500	$126,272	$3,622

I think I can safely say that this was one of the worst debt situations I had ever encountered, an extreme example. This was a couple out of control, so bitten by "The E Factor" that they had racked-up personal debts of $65,272. Bill and Sharon were locked into a lifetime of payments because their total income did not allow them to make more than the lowest possible payment on any of their debts, including their mortgage.

They had used most of the $49,500 in open-ended credit available to them to purchase every conceivable toy and trinket. They also used the credit to subsidize payments to other creditors because their budget was awash in red ink. Already into their forties, their prospects for a comfortable retirement were bleak, if not mathematically impossible. What's more, they only had a small amount of equity in their property and could not borrow more to consolidate debts. They were, in fact, maxed out.

How does Bill's short-term theory look to you now? Had Bill and Sharon exercised discipline, and set the amortization lower with a higher payment when they got the mortgage, they would not have had as much disposable income with which to incur personal debt. In addition, had they set their mortgage up properly, with a shorter amortization period, they would have had more equity in their home to help bail them out in an emergency. Since rates had gone up, their next renewal would have only served to increase an already crushing burden of monthly payments. In fact, they couldn't afford to lock in at a higher rate and feed their children at the same time. Their propensity for instant gratification had taken all their options away from them.

This is a very sad story. But it serves to illustrate that a one-size-fits-all theory with respect to length of term cannot possibly work.

In too many cases, these theories act against the consumer's best interests.

Now, there are times when a short term might be warranted, such as when market rates are high and obviously on a downward trend. But the question for anyone considering a short term or variable rate mortgage must ask themselves is this: can you afford to lose?

Most people can't and therefore I usually recommend longer terms, which give more protection against rate escalation. In my experience, the only people who successfully play the rate game with short terms are those in higher income brackets with little debt and lots of equity who have already reduced amortization. I still don't necessarily agree with gambling the home against the market, but these people can afford to be wrong. Most of the bottom 80 percent of the population can't.

While affordability is a key question, so is comfort. Some people can play the rate market, even a volatile market, without ever breaking a sweat. They have ice water running through their veins. If rates go up, they just pay the higher payment until rates go down.

Other people jump onto the short-term bandwagon worry about it constantly. They find themselves checking the newspaper every day. Rates are on their mind when they go to sleep, and they are still there when they wake up.

These people are prone to panic when rates rise. They then lock themselves in to a higher rate than they could have received had they locked in to a long term in the first place. This is analagous to a nervous mutual fund investor who panics when the market goes down, and instead of waiting it out, decides to sell – at a loss!

When I was taking mutual fund courses, they drove the point home that comfort level was a major factor when helping a client select an investment. If the client was nervous about the stock market, then they should be steered towards something safer like money market funds or bonds or term deposits, even though the returns could be less.

Your mortgage is an investment. Your strategy should be just as carefully thought out as any other investment strategy.

The Longer Terms

It's difficult to make long-range plans today considering the uncertainties we face in the job market. Nevertheless, we must have long-term goals and strategies that are part and parcel of an overall financial plan.

In essence, long-term mortgages–from five years up–provide greater protection from rate escalation and higher payments, which can upset a financial plan. Having the security that your mortgage payment won't increase is worth something because the road to retirement contains many bumps and potholes. Over the course of a working life, studies now indicate a person could well have as many as five different occupations, and who-knows-how-many jobs. When income is interrupted or reduced, the last thing you need is a pending mortgage renewal with a 2 or 3 percent rate hike. The markets can be very volatile from time to time, and having a mortgage renewal due in the middle of the fury can be unsettling, if not actually disastrous. The slightly higher payment, which is inherent in a longer-term, is an insurance policy against market volatility and an investment in your future.

For first-time homebuyers, many of whom are already financially squeezed, a longer term is made mandatory by mortgage default insurers because these buyers need the protection. The current minimum is three years, and I believe it should be five. In fact, anyone who cannot afford to have a healthy increase in payments should take a longer term. It just makes sense, because it provides more security.

Personally, when rates are near or at the bottom of the cycle, I recommend the 10-year term if it fits into the overall financial plan of the client. The 10-year term provides a great deal of protection against rate escalation. In addition, in the event rates did rise at time of renewal, the mortgage balance on the tenth anniversary would be lower than on the fifth, particularly when a shorter amortization was selected. As a result, the borrower would be in a much better position to deal with the increase at that point. Also, the financial plan, after ten years, should be much more fully developed than after five, and for this reason, the overall financial ability to withstand a rate increase should be much better. (That's should be.)

If during the 10-year term you decide to sell your home and buy another, you could port your mortgage (that is, bring the unpaid balance with you to the new location with the same rate and payments).

There is one caution with respect to longer terms. If you intend to sell, and not buy again, before the third anniversary on a mortgage, and rates have gone down since your mortgage was granted, you could be in for a very large interest-differential penalty. If you sell after the third anniversary on a default-insured mortgage, the insurer protects you from this kind of penalty, by limiting the lenders to charging you only a three-month interest penalty. So before you take a 10-year term, please get some sound financial advice, and have your plans in place. Nobody can predict the future, however, so your final decision, no matter how well thought out, is always a bit of a gamble.

Perhaps you have heard stories about the rate market of the early 1980s. Hopefully, you were not involved in it. For those who do not remember or haven't heard, mortgage interest rates rose well into the teens, and the prime rate went above the 20 percent mark. People lost their homes and businesses failed.

For me, the most painful thing was to see bank customers dropping off the keys to their homes. Their five-year renewals were coming due just as the rates were peaking, and they could no longer afford the payments. In retrospect, and with the benefit of perfect hindsight, they would have been better served by the 10-year term, as rates had gone from 8 or 9 percent five years before to 14, 15 or 16 percent on renewal.

However, term selection was not the only mistake people made. While the media tends to blame the loss of homes during that time only on the rates, many people exacerbated their problems with debts they had incurred since they had become homeowners.

Rate Negotiation

Now that you have selected a term, and are confident you can afford the payments based on the bank's posted rate, it's time to enter into rate negotiation.

You may want to start by allowing the lender to take the lead. You can ask a leading question that will cause the lender to go into presentation mode. After all, the lender has seen the quality of the product you are selling and just may be willing to buy it right then and there!

What's the leading question that you can ask that can springboard your application into mortgage heaven? How, in other words, do you find out how many cookies there are in the cookie jar? I heard a good answer to this recently:

Turning the Tables

I had occasion to attend a monthly luncheon meeting that was a gathering of self-employed business people. At each of these meetings there is a guest speaker. The speakers commonly talk about how they started their businesses and how they made them successful. They also give detailed accounts of the pitfalls they had to endure along the way.

On this day, a man who had started a construction business addressed the group. He was an immigrant to Canada, and spoke very broken English – he was difficult to understand at times. He began to tell a story of how he successfully obtained financing for his business. Business loans are *extremely* difficult to come by, and the man told about being rejected for financing, while some people in the room started making some very negative comments about banks.

I was able to sit there, taking this all in like a fly on the wall, because nobody knew who I was, or anything about my background. It was very interesting indeed to hear the comments, and none of them really surprised me.

In any event, the man, after being turned down a few times for a business loan, decided to take a different approach when he visited the next lender. He asked the lender, "Why should I deal with your bank? What can you offer me another bank can't?" With this approach, the man caught the banker completely off guard and put him into presentation mode. The lender immediately started to sell the man on the idea of dealing with that bank even before he had seen his application. As a result, the man won the approval for his financing and at a better price than he ever imagined.

The room erupted with applause.

Can you figure out what happened here? The man had previously approached lenders with his hat in his hand, in a very sheepish way, very modest, very humble and probably displaying an extreme lack of confidence. Of course, the lenders picked up on this, and since they weren't challenged, they were comfortable in playing it safe and declining the applicant.

By contrast, on the last visit, the man entered the banker's office with confidence and took charge of the situation right away. Instead of interviewing the man, the banker found himself being interviewed. What did that do? It neutralized the banker's power, and actually placed the power into the hands of the client.

You must understand, the power the bank and the banker seem to possess is an illusion. It is the people who hold the power, and so it should always be.

I can't say that this particular approach will always yield a positive result. Certainly not. It's just another tool to have in your repertoire.

If by this point the lender has not offered a rate that is palatable to you, you will need to negotiate further. Remember, rate is only one component of the cost of the mortgage.

With respect to rate negotiation, you should know that most lenders view rate discounts as risk relative. Yes, your presentation and preparation mean a lot, however the quality of your product and the degree of risk the bank believes it is taking on in lending to you will determine how low a rate you will receive. I can't give you a specific formula for product quality, but I can give you a general set of guidelines.

Generally speaking, your negotiation for a lower rate will be more successful if:

- **you have spent many years in your job. (a trick in modern times!)**
- **you have an unblemished credit history.**
- **your affordability ratios are well within the guidelines.**
- **you have a large down payment (applicants with the largest down payments tend to get the back room rates.)**
- **your mortgage is $100,000 or more. (the smaller the mortgage, the smaller the profit. Consequently, lenders are not motivated to discount rates where their profits are already challenged.)**

To the degree that any of the aforementioned is lacking, your rate will tend to go up from wherever the bottom has been set. There is a price to be paid for poor credit. There is a price to be paid for instability (even though the banks contribute to it themselves with layoffs). There is also a price to be paid for the increased risk that comes from a small down payment.

Of course the other factor to consider is competition, which sometimes blows the doors off of reason. If you are shopping more than one financial institution, you may find them in a bidding war over your business. That's not a bad place to be. Let each lender you visit know you are shopping around and encourage each to compete for your business. Tell them you know your qualifications are very good and you're shopping for the best deal.

The Skilled Negotiator

One day I received a call from a woman looking for a mortgage.

"My name is Shauna Peters. My husband and I are in the market for a mortgage and we would like to make an appointment with you."

"Fine, Mrs. Peters. When would you like to come in?"

"One p.m. Thursday. We have another appointment with a bank at 11:30, so we should be able to be there by 1."

"I see, yes 1 p.m. would be fine. This will be a day of shopping for you, will it?"

"It certainly will. We will have five appointments all together. We'll be exhausted once it's all over.

"Mrs. Peters, do you mind me asking when is your last appointment of the day?"

"Not at all. It's at 4 p.m."

"I see. Would it be too much to ask if I could see you after that, say at 5 or 5:15? I would like to be your last appointment of the day. I'll have some refreshments here for you. How's that?"

To my surprise, Mrs. Peters agreed to my request without asking the reason for it.

At 5 p.m. Thursday afternoon, Mrs. Peters and her husband came to my office loaded down with information from four of my strongest competitors. I knew I had my work cut out for me.

"We have some very good mortgage offers here," Mrs. Peters said.

"I can well imagine. Let's see what you've got. I'll compare every single point from each of the four lenders to our mortgage product, and then you'll have all the information you need to make a decision."

We remained there for one hour, poring over every single mortgage offer, comparing it to the product I was selling. At the end of an hour I had won (and earned) their business. They did in fact receive the best deal in town.

My purpose in scheduling myself as the Peters' last appointment of the day was to be able to see every other offer they had, and to be able to sell against it. Had I been lender number one or two, I would not have had the advantage of knowing what the other lenders were offering, and in all likelihood would have lost the business.

Would you care to guess how many calls I received during my twenty-five years in lending in which a customer let me know I was just one appointment in a crowd and would have to work for their business? Just one. Sad, but true!

The mortgage shopping day of Mr. and Mrs. Peters was the finest I had ever been involved with. They were extremely well versed in mortgages, and they tested my abilities right to the extremes. I wasn't threatened by that. I always enjoyed the heat of competitive battle. There were several points during that hour when I thought all was lost, but my own degree of preparation made a difference.

As rare an event as this may be, it is exactly what I recommend. It is very acceptable to let a competing lender know what kind of offers you have had, after he or she has made their first offer to you. It's all part of the negotiation process. If you succeed in starting a bidding war and wind up with a rate so low it's beyond reason, that is for the lender to have to explain to his or her boss. You can go out and celebrate!

Mr. and Mrs. Peters did one more thing I fully support. They began their shopping day with the bank where they did all their business, where they already had a first mortgage. This bank quoted them a rate representing the full-posted rate for the term they had selected, with no discount at all. Perhaps they were oblivious to the fact Mr. and Mrs. Peters were going shopping. Obviously, the "We've Got 'Em" factor was at work here.

Mr. and Mrs. Peters handled this situation in exactly the right way. Their bank paid the price for taking their business for granted by losing it. However, once again, Mr. and Mrs. Peters are in the minority, because most consumers would have taken the best competitive offer they could find right back to their bank, and requested they match it. In many cases the bank will.

You deserve better than that. You deserve the benefit of a new relationship in which the bank demonstrates a keen and genuine interest in your business. And should that relationship ever be taken for granted, you owe it to yourself to find a new banker once more. Because even in the best of times business relationships can only be considered to be temporary. I learned that time and time again over the course of my career. Seniority means nothing.

After using the various negotiating strategies, and showing the lender your competitive mortgage offers, if you do not receive the desired response, it may be time to suggest a rate yourself, somewhere below the best rates you see advertised. Sometimes lenders will horse trade for the back-room rates by offering additional discounts in exchange for a greater percentage of your banking business.

For example, if you agree to move your regular banking business there, that could be worth something. If you have investments at competing financial institutions and agree to transfer some or all of it over, that can influence things as well. The transfer of business allows the bank to recover some of the losses incurred by giving you a back-room rate.

You must weigh this kind of thing carefully, however. First, is it going to be worth it for you to transfer your business over in exchange for the extra discount the lender is offering? Is the new financial institution as competitive as the one with which you are now dealing in regard to these other products? Will the degree to which you have to upset your investments be greater than the impact of the further reduced mortgage rate?

After weighing these and any other considerations you may have, the final decision is yours. However, I would suggest you not flatly reject the deal being offered by the lender even if you are unhappy with it. You want to walk out of there with a mortgage offer (in writing, please!) because it can be used as a bargaining device at your next sales meeting.

Sometimes bankers will give you a written mortgage offer that does not mention the pricing. They may have communicated that to you orally. This is the lender's attempt to diminish the competitive value of the mortgage offer in your hands so it cannot be used as a bargaining tool down the road.

The problem is you absolutely need a full offer in writing. If this is the offer you are ultimately going to accept, you require the rate to be guaranteed for at least sixty to ninety days so that you can buy a home or finalize the mortgage transaction before rates go up. Any lender worth his salt will give it to you in writing. It is the negative-power bankers who will attempt to short-circuit your mortgage shopping initiative. Avoid them like the plague!

Amortization

I know we have talked about the benefits of reduced amortization at length, however its importance as the most significant factor in the cost of borrowing does make it worth some further discussion.

You should always select the lowest amortization you can reasonably afford. Having your mortgage paid off in the least possible time is worth a fortune to you. Reduction of the cost of borrowing is not the only consideration here, though. Ask yourself, How old do I want to be when I finally pay off my mortgage?

For some people, that question is a wake-up call. They tend to automatically set mortgage amortization at twenty-five years, not thinking that this may well carry them into years when they would not be comfortable making mortgage payments. It may also take them into years when they wouldn't be able to afford their mortgage payments should an interruption or reduction in income occur.

As I said before, the road to retirement does contain some bumps and potholes. You simply cannot assume everything will go smoothly through forty years of working life. It is best to plan for the upsets, because in most cases, especially in today's environment, they will occur.

Here are some good questions to ask yourself:

- **At what age do I want to be free of mortgage payments?**
- **Is the amortization I am selecting going to encroach on the reduced-income years of my retirement?**
- **How much will my income be in retirement according to my financial plan? Could I afford mortgage payments based on this income?**
- **What are my long-term prospects for continued employment?**
- **Can I always count on being healthy?**

Your youthful years, your productive years, are the years in which you should attack your mortgage and all of your personal debt as though it were your mortal enemy. If you do this, you'll be able to enjoy your retirement years in comfort and peace. Your assault on debt will reduce the harmful effects of job loss, ill health, marital disharmony and other negative factors, which tend to increase in risk with the passing of time, and impair your ability to make debt payments.

In all too many cases, I have seen the tragic results of letting debt linger. When a reduction in income occurs, people who have been making the lowest payments possible are ill prepared to handle it. In some cases they are forced to borrow more to bail themselves out, to salvage whatever equity in their homes they have to re-mortgage and keep the borrowing bandwagon going in perpetuity. Some are caught dead to rights by their actions and lose everything. So please, reduce that amortization!

It may interest you to know that 95 percent of all 25-year amortizations are set that way unnecessarily. Most people who can qualify for a mortgage in the first place, do not require a 25-year amortization. They must qualify at the posted rate anyway. (If you can't afford the payments based on the posted rate, you are buying too much house!) In most cases, anyone who does qualify can get a rate discount of at least 25 basis points which should be converted, not to lower payments, but to reduced amortization.

Based on the highest payment you can reasonably afford (you don't want to be house poor) and the rate you have just negotiated, ask the lender what is the amortization. This is a reversal of the way this is usually done, but it is also the right way to set amortization.

Normally, lenders calculate mortgages in the following manner:

Mortgage Amount	Rate	Amortization	Payment
$100,000	7%	25 years	?

This is the way most bank mortgage systems are set up – to solve for the payment as the only variable. That means the payment is the unknown factor. However, as a wise and educated consumer, you know what payment is so you want the lender to do the calculation like this:

Mortgage Amount	Rate	Payment	Amortization
$100,000	7%	$700.42	?

Here, the amortization is the variable, and the final result of the calculation. There's only one problem. Because most computer systems today are programmed to calculate only the payment variable, if your lender has not received any training in mortgage finance (most have not) he or she may be unable to make that calculation. What they might do is try and arrive at it by trial and error, playing with the computer to get a payment close to the one you want.

If you have calculated that your maximum payment affordability is $800 (before taxes and heat) on a mortgage of $100,000, including mortgage default premiums, if any, and the rate is 7 percent compounded semi-annually and not in advance, the calculation would look something like this:

Mortgage Amount	Rate	Payment	Amortization
$100,000	7%	$800.00	18.44 years

Most computer systems will not accept part of a month or year, so just adjust the amortization to 18 years and recalculate the payment. That should be acceptable to the lender, as long as the payments fall within their affordability guidelines.

If this $800 payment really and truly fits into your financial plan, is there any good reason you can think of why you should take a 25-year amortization? By doing things this way, you have just shaved 6.56 years off your amortization. Congratulations! What's the value of that? Multiply 6.56 years by 12 months by $700.42, and you find that you have saved yourself $55,137.06.

You can further increase your savings by taking accelerated bi-weekly payments. What would be that effect on this same mortgage? Your amortization would be further reduced to 15.78 years! You will have now shaved 9.22 years off your amortization. What's the value of that? Multiply 9.22 by 12 by $700.42. That equals $77,494.47!

Remember, lower amortization is absolutely critical to your financial future. Had you allowed the lender to automatically calculate your payment the conventional way, it would have looked like this:

$$\$100,000 \times 7\% \times 25 \text{ Years} = \$700.42$$

Your payment would have remained at $700.42, a difference of approximately $50 or $100 per bi-weekly period. Is it possible to lose $100 in the family budget in a given month? For many people, it's possible to lose more than that. So if you have the means, why not take an ounce of discipline and invest it in your future?

Now, lets look at these two mortgages in terms of their overall cost of borrowing.

Factors	Mortgage with Payment of $700.42 Monthly	Same Mortgage with Payment of $800, Reducing the Amortization
Mortgage Amount	$100,000	$100,000
Total Interest Charged	$110,126	$77,000
Total Mortgage To Be Repaid	$210,126.	$177,000
Difference		$33,126

This comparison is based on two fully amortized mortgages. The rate you negotiate on your next term may slightly alter these figures.

It *does* make a difference to look at the overall cost of borrowing as a dollar value instead of a rate, doesn't it? The number of dollars paid out is the true cost of the mortgage, and most people lose sight of that fact by concentrating too much on the rate of interest.

You now have all of the components for the lender to write you a mortgage offer. Please ensure that the rate is guaranteed for at least sixty days or longer, should you be able to negotiate it. Some lenders will go to ninety days and a few beyond that.

Somewhere in the course of your sales meeting with the lender you should find out about the additional aspects of their mortgage products as we have discussed:

- **Flexible prepayment features like annual increase in payments, flexible double ups and lump sum anniversary payment**
- **Accelerated weekly or bi-weekly payments**
- **Portability (the ability to take your mortgage to a new property)**

- **Assumability (whether someone could take over your mortgage if you wanted to sell - not always recommended)**
- **Fees**
- **Penalties (to be discussed in a later chapter - most lenders have the same penalty structure)**
- **Cost of life insurance (recommended)**

Make notes, keeping them in a folder, concerning all the information gathered from each lender. Store your mortgage offers in this same folder.

I should give you one more bit of consumer advice on the negotiation process. It is very possible that during the course of your negotiation, you noticed that the lender was pushing you towards a certain term or mortgage product irrespective of your financial needs.This is because lenders sometimes dictate terms.

Term Dictation

You already know that mortgage-default insurers make it mandatory that you take a longer term if you are a first-time buyer with only the minimum down payment. In the same way, the lender may also dictate the term if they have a concern about your credit and borrowing habits. But in the absence of any of these factors, why would a lender try to steer you in a particular direction and even dictate the term? It could be that your lender is working on commission.

There is a disturbing trend in the financial services industry to have financial advisors work on commission. Today, their incomes may be derived from a commission supplement over and above an annual salary, or be entirely derived from commission, with no salary at all. Such an arrangement places the financial advisor under extreme pressure to sell more products at the highest possible prices just to be able to make a living.

Once again, this is not to fault the employees of financial institutions. Commission is a way of reducing expenses by only paying for productivity. In some industries it works. However, in an institution where financial advice is being rendered, with hundreds of thousands or even millions of dollars at stake, it is practically impossible for any institution to claim they are acting in the best interests of their clients in a commission environment. There will always be some employees who abuse the system by steering a customer into a borrowing or investment product that isn't good for them, just so the advisor can make more money. If times are tough, even the most honest individual can act irresponsibly.

Often the commission structures will pay the lender more for a longer mortgage term sold. They can also earn more by selling additional products like life insurance and other bank services. They earn less by giving in to your demands for a lower rate.

I am certainly not saying that financial advisors don't have a right to earn a living. It could be that what they are selling you lines up just exactly with your needs. However, please remember, you have the absolute right to make your decision and select the product that is right for you, regardless of any commission the advisor will earn.

I would recommend that sometime in the sales meeting you ask the lender if he or she is on commission. If the lender refuses to answer it may be advisable to eliminate that financial institution from competition for your business. There are enough lenders around who still pay their employees a salary without the possible added bias of commission.

Perhaps this question should be asked after you have had a chance to build a rapport, and after the lender has already agreed to your terms. In this way, you can look back on the advice you received and decide if it was biased.

Another reason a lender may attempt to influence your decision on term as well as amortization is that the lender may be selling your mortgage. This is another topic not often discussed with consumers. The lender may indeed be selling your mortgage. They have the right to do that – mortgages are fully assignable debt instruments and a lender could sell your mortgage to your mother-in-law (heaven forbid!) if he wanted to.

Why do lenders sell mortgages? Well, in the first place it's profitable - they make money off the sale – and it helps the lender stay liquid. Some smaller financial institutions, like credit unions, may not have sufficient funds on deposit from their own internal investors to engage in mortgage lending in the communities they serve. So, they sell the mortgage to an outside investor or group of investors as soon as it is funded. The whole process is invisible to the mortgage borrower. You still make your payments to the lender, but little do you realize that they are forwarding all payments to a central authority that collects them on behalf of a pool of mortgage investors.

The investors in these pools may have specific requirements as to the type of mortgages they will buy. In the case of mortgage-backed securities (MBS), there are certain programs into which a lender can enter for the sale of mortgages. One program might demand mortgages of either three or five-year terms, and no less than 22 years in amortization. If the lender writes too many mortgages that the MBS program won't buy, the lender may run into trouble by committing more money than the statutes that govern that lender will allow. The lender could run out of money to lend altogether.

If you are in search of a reduced amortization, a lender in the MBS program may try to steer you into a 25-year amortization without telling you the reason. (They may just tell you outright, but this is rare.) Be aware that you may be getting advice that is not in your best interests.

It is usually the smaller, poorly capitalized financial institutions that tend to be governed by the mortgages they can sell. While the major banks also participate in the MBS program, they have far more resources, and term influence is less likely to be a factor at the branch level. However, a commissioned employee is more likely to be found in the major banks. There are always trade-offs.

When you get home after a day of mortgage shopping, you will have quite a task at hand to pore over the contents of your folder, and to read all of the brochures and pamphlets you picked up along the way. Now, the final decision is yours. When you have decided, sign the mortgage offer you have selected and return it to the lender so that they will know you will be using their services. They need your signed commitment to hold the money for you.

-11-

Hidden Dangers in the Pre-Approval Process

"Set the foot down with distrust on the crust of the world — it is thin."
— Edna St. Vincent Millay, Huntsman, What Quarry?

Having come through the pre-approval process, you may now have a piece of paper in your hands called a pre-approved mortgage certificate. It means that you have taken the first step to final approval, but further steps must be taken, and we are going to discuss them in this chapter.

Your pre-approved mortgage certificate will contain a set of conditions you must fulfil before final approval is granted. If you followed the advice in the previous chapter and brought all of the information recommended to your sales meeting with the lender, the certificate should state that final approval is subject to these certain conditions:

- **Appraisal of the property**
- **Insurer approval if required**
- **The lender pulling their own credit report to confirm your credit score is within their lending guidelines**
- **The lender's receipt of your offer to purchase the home you want to buy**
- **A gift letter, if any portion of your down payment is gifted from a relative**

You should have already proven to the lender:
> **• Your ability to repay the mortgage with your proof-of-income documentation**
> **• Your intent to repay with the copy of the credit report you provided**
> **• Your ability to make the necessary down payment (perhaps with the exception of the gifted portion) with the copies of your bank and other investment statements**

There can be more conditions based on your own personal financial situation, but these are the most common.

If any portion of your down payment is gifted, please make sure the gifter gives you the money for deposit into your bank account before an offer is made, and preferably before your first meeting with the lender. This is a requirement of the mortgage-default insurer.

At this stage the quality of the work you have done and the energy you have invested should make the entire home buying process flow more smoothly. The last thing you want, with all of the decisions you have to make about the home itself, is to be faced with a laborious mortgage search process. You've already done that. You've already provided the documentation they required, and the lender has given you the pre-approval certificate free of any conditions pertaining to that documentation. You have done it the right way. You can now go shopping for a home and be confident of final approval.

You would not believe, however, how many people skip all, or part of the pre-approval process. They do not invest the time and energy you have and wind up facing the consequences. It's just another example of "The E Factor" at work. The fastest and seemingly easiest way is often the road to failure.

The pre-approval certificate of the average mortgage applicant will have all kinds of conditions on it:

> **• A letter from the employer confirming income, employment status, or if self employed, financial statements and notices of assessment going back three years**
> **• T4s from the last three years**
> **• A current pay stub**
> **• Proof of down payment, including bank statements**

from the last three months, or documented proof from any other source
- **A credit report satisfactory for the bank's purposes**
- **Appraisal of the property, if required**
- **Insurer approval, if required**
- **A gift letter, if required**

In other words, this mortgage applicant wandered into a banker's office with no documentation at all. Therefore, this applicant was given *an entirely worthless pre-approval certificate.*

The applicant failed at the time of the meeting to prove to the lender his or her *ability* and *intent* to repay. As a result, the lender handed the applicant a pre-approval certificate subject to absolutely everything. In essence, all it did was reserve a block of money at a certain rate for a certain time just in case the applicant ever did prove he or she could qualify for a mortgage.

This home hunter, carrying the worthless pre-approval certificate will now seek out a real-estate agent, tell the agent they have been pre-approved, spend days, weeks or even months looking for a home, write the offer and then get turned down by the bank. Why?

Thanks to the lack of preparation by the mortgage applicant and his delay or failure to satisfy the conditions of the pre-approval certificate once it was issued, the bank waited until the offer was written to begin the qualification process. The mortgage applicant was approved only in his or her own mind!

I see cases like this one every single week! However, it is not completely the fault of the mortgage applicant. Let's be fair, the bank should have informed the client that this was a very conditional approval. In most cases, the lender will not do this. They leave it to the client to read the certificate, which is often very ambiguously worded, and people, especially first time homebuyers, just do not understand all of the ramifications involved.

I believe any truly professional lender has a moral obligation to serve their clients well, to educate them about the transaction they are about to enter into, to warn them about the pitfalls and to guide them through to the end. Now I must say that even a truly professional lender, even with the best of intentions, cannot guarantee there will be no bumps in the road if the borrower is not equally committed to doing his or her part. If things are to go smoothly, it takes the combined efforts of the lender and the borrower.

Since I see so many of these failed attempts at homeownership, I have a wealth of examples. Here is one cautionary tale:

The Story of Robert and Sandra

Robert and Sandra visited their bank one day to inquire about a mortgage. They were about to contact a real-estate agent and go shopping for their first home. They had saved their own down payment, a two-year process.

The lender at the bank, Vera, interviewed them for about ten minutes, and then in a very hurried fashion, hurled a piece of paper across the desk stating they had been pre-approved.

"When you find a house just bring us the offer," Vera said. With that, the meeting ended and Robert and Sandra left the bank walking on air. They could not believe how easy it was to get pre-approved. As they looked at their certificate they found they had been pre-approved for a mortgage of $110,000 at a rate of 7 percent per annum. They were very excited and eager to begin their home hunting expedition.

Robert contacted Jim, a real-estate agent who had acted for his family before. He told Jim he was pre-approved for a mortgage, discussed the price range they wanted to buy in and arranged for a meeting. Robert and Sandra would begin their search for the perfect home on the weekend.

As it turned out the search lasted three weeks. Between doing drive-bys and actual viewings they had looked at over seventy properties. They were exhausted, and so was their agent, but they had finally found exactly what they were looking for, their perfect home.

As instructed, Robert and Sandra made an appointment to see Vera with the accepted offer in hand. They had just five days to arrange financing according to the terms of their contract.

During the meeting Vera gave them a list of things that were needed to process the deal:

- **Letters of employment verification for both of them.**
- **Their T4s from the last taxation year.**
- **Current pay stubs for each.**
- **Proof of down payment – copies of their bank state-**

ments for the last three months, and their mutual fund statements from which a part of the down payment was coming.
• **A cheque for $175 for the appraisal and $75 for the default insurance application fee.**

They ended the meeting, with Vera vowing to take care of everything. She told them not to worry, just to round up the required documentation.

Robert and Sandra left the bank somewhat in shock, and in a panic over what they now realized was still to be done. They wished the lender had told them all of this in the first place and yet, upon reviewing the pre-approval certificate again, they realized they had not paid much attention to the conditions. Time was now of the essence and according to instructions from the lender, they had to have this information within four days to allow the final approval process to take place. If they failed, their exhausting house-hunt would be all for nothing. Their offer would expire, and a back-up offer would take precedence. Another couple could buy their dream home right out from under them.

Robert was able to get his documentation within one day. He was lucky. Sandra, however, was not so lucky. Her employer said it would take a week to get the letter, as it had to be ordered from Human Resources in Montreal. Moreover, Sandra was not very good at keeping records. She could not find her T4s, and at the request of the lender, had to rush down to Revenue Canada to retrieve copies of her income tax notices of assessment as further proof of income.

What a hassle. She pleaded with her boss to find a way to speed up the process. The boss was sympathetic, and over the course of the next few days, managed to convince head office to move quickly. The letter arrived on the fourth day, late in the afternoon.

Unable to leave work early, Sandra faxed all of the documentation to the lender right from her place of employment. Robert's documentation was already there. He had delivered it on his lunch hour on the second day.

They had made the deadline! What a relief. It had been a very scary experience but Robert and Sandra promised each other this would never happen again. When they bought their next home they would take better care to read the fine print and to prepare ahead of time to prevent such a panic situation. They went to sleep that night confident the purchase of their new home would proceed just fine, as it was now in the capable hands of their lender.

It was noon of the fifth day, the last day allowed for financing. Jim took a call from the listing agent of the property on which Robert and Sandra had made their offer.

"What's going on, Jim? My vendors are getting nervous. Are your clients going to complete this deal?"

"Yes. I'm sure they are. They should receive word from the bank today. I think they were a little late in getting all their documents, but it should be fine."

Jim thought he should put in a call to the bank to make sure everything was okay. He couldn't reach Robert and Sandra, as they were both on their lunch hours. He knew the lender, and was confident he could find out how the deal was progressing.

"Hi, Vera, it's Jim. You're working on my deal for Robert and Sandra. How's it going?"

"Well, they've been turned down."

"What? What do you mean turned down? What's going on there? You pre-approved them!"

"Jim, all I can tell you is their application does not meet our lending requirements. I can't give you any more details. It's confidential. If they want to know the reason, have them call me."

Jim was furious. How could this happen? Three weeks, seventy homes including twenty-eight showings, and now this? What would Robert and Sandra say? As much as he hated to do it, he had to make the call.

"Hello, Sandra, it's Jim. I've got some bad news. I called the bank today to find out how your mortgage was coming along, I couldn't reach you so I called them."

Sandra could sense the tension in Jim's voice. It sounded as though he was shaking. "What's the matter, Jim? What did they say?"

"Your application was turned down, Sandy. I'm sorry. Maybe you should call the bank and find out what's going on."

"What reason did they give, Jim?" By now, Sandra was shaking too.

"They just said it was confidential and that if you wanted to know the reason you could call them. I'm sorry, Sandra. I don't know what to say. I don't see how this could happen after you were pre-approved."

"I don't know either, Jim, but I'm sure going to find out. I'll call you back!"

By this time, Sandra's sense of shock and disbelief was turning into anger. She called Vera right away.

"Vera? Hi, this is Sandra. Jim said you have some news for us?"

"Yes. The bank is unable to process your application."

"Why is that?"

"Your credit report was unsatisfactory. You have some collections and a judgement against your record."

"I do not! I pay my bills on time. Who placed collections on my record?"

"If you want to get more information you can contact the credit bureau yourself. I can't give you the specifics. If you get it straightened out, come back and see us. We'll be happy to try again for you."

Sandra hung up the phone, and called Robert to break the news. Robert was furious, but he pledged to help Sandra fix the problem. In the meantime, Sandra had no choice but to call Jim and let him know they wouldn't be proceeding with the offer.

This is a sad story, isn't it? Unfortunately, stories just like this one are repeated each and every day in every city, town and municipality across the country. The tendency people have to procrastinate sometimes has very negative consequences.

Let's examine this story for a moment. Each party made at least one error or oversight along the way. In fact, they all share in the blame. Consider:

The Lender

Vera failed to give her clients any kind of professional counselling. She knew they were first-time homebuyers but she was busy that day and rushed the interview. Besides, in her mind Robert and Sandra had not made an offer yet, nor had they brought documentation with them, so there was lots of time. In addition, Vera thought there was a chance Robert and Sandra would go mortgage shopping elsewhere, so she wasn't going to put any more energy into the deal until she saw an offer. Consequently, Vera did not request a credit report.

When the offer was finally delivered, Vera still did not request a credit report. With five days allowed she thought she still had lots of time. Why rush?

Vera had actually gone home early on the day that Sandra had faxed the documentation, the afternoon of the fourth day. Vera was a part-time employee. She was not scheduled to return to work until noon the next day. She had just pulled the credit report and received a rejection notice from the computer when Jim called to check on the progress.

Vera did not offer to help Sandra straighten things out with the credit bureau.

The Real-Estate Agent

Jim had the presence of mind to intervene on Robert and Sandra's behalf in calling the bank. That's good. However, had he asked to see their pre-approval certificate in the first place, he would have known it was very incomplete, and could have warned them. While I am not placing the burden of responsibility on Jim's shoulders, I believe agents should be more actively involved and knowledgeable about financing issues. They would certainly save time and money by not working with people until they were truly qualified. Only a slight slap on the wrist here for Jim.

Robert and Sandra

Robert and Sandra failed to prepare adequately for their sales meeting with the lender. They had not taken along the documentation they required, thus, the lender really did not take them seriously.

Sandra's poor record keeping caught up with her and caused delay.

They failed to determine the level of experience of the lender. Vera was only a part-time staffer, just learning about mortgages. Vera's supervisor had been on holidays during that week.

Sandra should have put in a call to Vera on the fourth day when she was faxing the documents to make sure she had received them. Sandra had no way of knowing if these important documents actually found their way to Vera.

Both Robert and Sandra failed to obtain a copy of their credit report on an annual basis. Had she been monitoring her credit report as I recommended, she would have known a year earlier that some negative information had found its way onto her credit history.

Robert and Sandra committed the greatest error of all – they failed to shop for a mortgage. Vera gave them a pre-approval for the highest market rate with no consideration of a discount. (this is not Vera's fault; Robert and Sandra didn't ask. Vera is paid to make a profit.) In addition, had Robert and Sandra shopped around, they might have encountered a better lender — a professional purebred lender, perhaps, who would have given them the guidance they needed.

Robert and Sandra could have and should have sought out information and advice on mortgages and real estate before setting off to buy a home. I can tell you from past experience, the most financially successful people read the books, take the lessons, listen to the tapes and do whatever else is necessary to get the information they need. That in itself should tell a story.

By the way, we are not finished with the story of Robert and Sandra. There's more!

The Story of Robert and Sandra (continued)

Sandra placed a call to Jim to give him the news that their offer was going to lapse.

"We can't do it, Jim."

"I'm sorry, Sandra. I feel really bad about this."

"Don't feel too bad, I'm going to get it straightened out once and for all. I'm going to call that credit bureau and give them a piece of my mind!"

"Wait, Sandra. Don't go at them with a temper. I've heard about things like this before and I think you should get some professional advice."

"From who? Someone like Vera?"

"No, no. I think you should go to a mortgage broker."

"A mortgage broker? What could they do for me, Jim?"

"Sandy, a mortgage broker deals with a great many lending institutions. They know most of the lenders and can find you a good one in a heartbeat."

"But what about my credit report?"

"The broker can help you with that too. Most brokers are also members of the credit bureau, and with their experience, they would be in a better position to talk to the bureau than you would."

"That sounds interesting. But how much does it cost?"

"The brokers get paid by the financial institutions to bring them your business. So in most cases there's no fee to the client at all. You get the benefit of their expertise and the lender pays. Why don't you let me put in a call for you?"

"Okay, Jim. I'm willing to try anything at this point."

Jim contacted a broker with whom he regularly did business, and later that day the broker called Sandra.

"Hi, Sandra! My name is Gord Jamieson. Jim asked me to give you a call. How are you?"

"Not very well, Gord. We lost the house."

"Wait a minute, Sandy. Jim tells me the second offer just fell through. That house is back on the market."

"What? You're kidding! Do you think we can still get it?"

"It's possible. But we have some work to do. I can't guarantee anything except that I will do my best for you."

"Thanks, Gord. How exactly do you work?"

"Well, Sandra, I'm a broker, so I deal with many different lenders."

"Like an insurance broker?"

"Exactly. An insurance broker writes policies for their customers and they choose from the best insurance companies, which meet the needs of the client. The client can shop rates through the one broker so its saves a lot of time and energy. Plus, the client gets the benefit of the independent insurance broker's expertise and unbiased advice as to which companies are the best. Then the companies pay a commission to the broker."

"Does your business work the same way?"

"You bet it does. We deal with about twenty different lenders who pay us a commission. In fact, the lenders actively seek us out because it allows them to obtain a large volume of mortgage business from just a few sources, like tapping into a pool of customers."

"So, if you are paid by the lender, aren't you working for the lender?"

"We do have to maintain a good working relationship with the lenders, of course. However, it is our mandate to represent the client's best interests without compromising the interests of the lending institution. I work for you. It's my job to get you a mortgage at the lowest possible cost. I take your application and package it for presentation to the lender. Then we send your application to the top three lenders we believe would approve it. Once it's approved, we negotiate the best rate for you and then you can choose the offer you like best. How does that sound?"

"That sounds great, Gord! Where do we go from here?"

"I have to get your financial information. I can come over and do that, or in the interest of time I can do it right over the phone."

"You'll come right to the house?"

"Yes, I make house calls too. What's your pleasure?"

"Well, I would like to get moving on it right away so maybe we can do this over the phone."

"Fine. Is Robert there?"

"Yes, he just got out of the shower."

The broker took the necessary financial information from Robert and Sandra, and had Sandra fax the documents he required. Within an hour, Gord called back.

"Sandra, I have your credit report here. Looks like there's been a computer foul-up. There's some negative information on it that I know isn't yours."

"How do you know that?"

"Well, there are a bunch of collections against you and a judgement. Then at the bottom is a record of all your payment history, and it's just perfect. Sandra, it's not very likely that a person with excellent credit history can also be a deadbeat. Doesn't wash."

"Why couldn't the bank see that?"

"Well, Vera's new. I know a few lenders over there and they're very good. You just approached the wrong lender. It can happen."

"Do you think you can do this for us, Gord?"

"I'm very confident. But remember, nothing is guaranteed until I have it in writing from a lender. Because I have to deal with the credit bureau, this could take a couple of days. So sit tight, and I'll be back to you as soon as I can."

When the conversation ended, Robert and Sandra were filled with a new sense of hope that they would finally be able to buy their new home. The following morning Gord called.

"Hello, Sandra?"

"Yes, Gord. Is there something wrong? You're calling early."

"There's nothing wrong, Sandy. Unless, of course you call an approved mortgage something wrong."

"We're approved?"

"You are definitely about to become a homeowner."

Sandra was ecstatic, "How did you do it?"

"There was a very obvious computer glitch at the credit bureau.

Someone else's information had found its way onto your file. The rep fixed it for me and sent me a new report. Then I sent your application around to a few lenders I know, and bingo. It was easy."

"Well, you certainly made it look easy, Gord! How can we ever thank you?"

"How about buying me a coffee and telling your friends about my services?"

"You've got it!"

"I need to come over and show you these offers so you can pick the one you like best. See you at 7 p.m.?"

"Yes, 7 p.m. is fine. You say *offers*, plural? How many are there, Gord?"

"Four. We've got some work to do, Sandy."

"That's incredible!"

"What's even more incredible is that one of them is from ABC Bank. I'll see you at 7."

Robert and Sandra did get their mortgage. They also were able to write a new offer on the home they had taken such great care to select. They are now living their dream. I love happy endings.

It does pay to have professional representation, independent of the financial institution, if you are not comfortable in handling the mortgage-shopping process yourself. Although following the advice in this book should serve most people well and help them yield excellent results, others will not be comfortable doing it on their own. They would be better off to seek the services of a professional mortgage broker.

I want to stress the importance of reading every word of your pre-approved mortgage certificate carefully. Some of them are very ambiguously worded in order to protect the rights of the lender (not the borrower). You may find yourself on the wrong end of a word game, if you are not careful.

Here is an example of a pre-approved mortgage certificate that contains a potentially misleading statement .

Pre-Approved Mortgage Certificate

We are pleased to confirm that you have been

**pre-approved for a mortgage from ABC Bank
in the amount of**

$ 100,000

**provided the home meets our residential mortgage
standards and maximum permitted loan amounts,
and interest rates do not exceed**

6.95 percent

**This is subject to the bank's receipt of: A satisfactory
appraisal; proof of income; a satisfactory credit report;
proof of down payment; mortgage insurer approval.**

Can you see anything wrong with this certificate, aside from the fact that the applicant has failed to meet any of the approval requirements? Here's a clue: what's the rate and for how long is it guaranteed?

There is no rate guarantee here whatsoever. None. The lender has simply stated the maximum rate the applicant could qualify for, and has left the door open for any pricing structure they want to apply when the client brings an offer. Since it may take a month or more to find a house, the client is exposed to interest-rate escalation during that period. If rates were to rise sharply during that period, it is very possible the client would no longer qualify for a mortgage.

People have a tendency to look at a document like this and think the rate has been pegged at 6.95 percent. It happens all the time. In fact, a certificate like this is so worthless, you could set up a pre-approved mortgage certificate stand and hand them out to passersby.

If there is anything to be learned here, it is this: never compromise the degree to which you prepare for a real-estate transaction. Let the buyer beware.

Finally, I should like to cover one last point with respect to pre-approval certificates, and the role they play in your offer to purchase.

Most real-estate agents will tell you that if you have been pre-approved, it carries weight with the vendor when you make an offer. For the most part, that's true, but only because vendors do not realize how meaningless most pre-approval certificates are. (Of course, if you followed the right steps in obtaining your pre-approval certificate, it would have meaning.)

There have been far too many cases where both the vendor and the buyer placed too much credence in the certificate. I have heard of cases in which a home buyer would make an unconditional offer on the strength of the pre-approval certificate. They thought the certificate represented a firm approval, and they failed to insert a financing clause in their offer as a condition to cover themselves. When the lender declined the mortgage application, the lawsuits began.

Making an unconditional offer is sometimes suggested to the buyer as a means of impressing a vendor. An unconditional offer is seen as a sign of strength, and is designed to make a vendor favour this offer over another that does have a financing clause. Perhaps the strength of the offer will even bring a more favourable price for the buyer. That's the theory. However, if you require financing to purchase your home *always* insert a financing clause and allow yourself a minimum of five working days to win final approval.

There can be some very serious ramifications that result from failing to perform specific actions outlined in a contract. If you make an unconditional offer, and are then declined for mortgage financing, the vendor may sue for damages. This is a very ugly situation, and it can be avoided by using good, common sense. If you have any doubts, consult your lawyer.

At this stage, we will assume you have made an offer that has been accepted and the bank has given you a letter of final approval with no conditions. Only one question remains: will your mortgage be funded?

Most mortgages reaching this point are successfully funded; the lender writes the cheque for your mortgage as promised. However, the lender can refuse to fund the mortgage under certain conditions, even if they have given you a final approval letter. If they suspect fraud, or come upon new information they had previously not discovered that leads them to believe the mortgage does not conform to their policies, they can and will withhold funds.

Always be completely honest in your dealings. A loan or some other form of obligation not declared in the initial interview can be enough to make a lender revoke their approval. And once again, that is when the lawyers become involved.

-12-

The Mortgage Closing

"I sincerely believe... that banking establishments are more dangerous than standing armies, and that the principle of spending money to be paid by posterity, under the name of funding, is but swindling futurity on a large scale." — *Thomas Jefferson.*

You will quite possibly be invited back to see your lender one last time, before your meeting at the lawyer's office. This exercise should be nothing more than a confirmation of the facts, as you already know them, with respect to the choices you've made on rate, term, etc. You can use the closing to confirm your final decision on things agreed to in the pre-approval process, such as life insurance, accelerated weekly or bi-weekly payments and other banking services.

It's important to have considered these matters, and, for all intents and purposes, to have your mind made up before you go into the closing with the lender. There are other things to do here that will warrant your full attention.

Here is a list of things that you may have to do during your mortgage closing:

- **Read and sign the final mortgage offer, making sure it is acccurate and in accordance with what you negotiated.**
- **Open new accounts, if you agreed to do so.**
- **Sign up for mortgage life insurance, if you opted to take it.**
- **Confirm decision on payment structure (weekly, bi-weekly, etc.).**
- **Present the lender with the name of your lawyer.**
- **Execute loan documents if a personal loan was granted in addition to the mortgage.**

All in all, there can be a lot to do during a closing, which can take up to one hour in some cases. It is absolutely essential that you be alert and allow no distractions in this meeting, because a mistake can cost you.

There is another purpose to the mortgage closing, and this is perhaps the most important one to the lender. It's an opportunity for the lender to sell you every service the bank has, if you don't already have it. It is a product sales-a-thon, pure and simple, and the stakes are very high for the lender.

Most financial institutions place great pressure on their employees to "cross-sell" services. In fact, the employee may be trying to meet a very aggressive set of goals. They may be paid a commission for additional services they sell. I mention this not to suggest it's either a good thing or a bad thing, but to make you aware of what is going on.

If you decide a particular service is right for you, by all means, buy it. However, I want you to know you should not feel unduly pressured by the lender, who may be trying to exert power over you, to buy into things you don't need or want. You have every right as a consumer to say no. That is, unless you have agreed to buy the services as part of the overall package the lender offered you.

Mortgage Life Insurance

Over the course of my career, upon hearing of the news of a borrower's death, I have occasionally had to inform a surviving spouse that they had no mortgage life insurance. It was a difficult experience for me but I can't even imagine how painful it must have been for the spouse. Not only were they widowed, but they were now solely responsible for the remaining mortgage payments. Sometimes this entailed literally years of unnecessary payments totalling tens of thousands of dollars, if not more than a hundred thousand dollars. It was all because at the mortgage closing, they had failed to see the value in paying a small additional premium for life-insurance coverage.

When I recall those experiences, I wonder why some people strenuously resist life insurance, especially when it is being offered to them at the affordable rates we have today. They seem to want to put it off, and by and large these same people tend to also be those most influenced by "The E Factor."

More often than not, when I bring up the subject of life insurance with a married couple, the wife is immediately interested. She looks over to her husband, signalling him to say yes, and he, almost invariably, will resist. Sometimes he will just let out a grunt, indicating they don't need life insurance. Other times, the wife will take command of the situation and say yes before the husband has had a chance to object. In any event, if there is to be an objector, it is usually the male partner. I won't speculate about the reasons for this, except to say it has been my experience that women, on average, seem to see the benefits of planning for the future more clearly than men.

Perhaps the most common excuse given for declining mortgage life insurance is "I'm insured at work." Really? Insured for what? The fact is most people are extremely *under-insured*, and those who rely on their insurance at work fail to consider what would happen if they lost their jobs. It's astonishing, considering all we have been through in the recent past, that people still take their jobs for granted.

I always recommend mortgage life-insurance coverage, especially for married couples. After the loss of the departed spouse's income, the widow or widower can ill afford to continue making mortgage payments. In the absence of coverage, spouses are often forced to sell the home to avoid a financial crisis. Unfortunately for all too many, the sale of the home *is* a financial crisis because much of the equity must go to repay debt.

There are three types of insurance most commonly used to insure mortgages. The first, and most popular type is offered by the lender.

Mortgage Life Offered by Lenders

Mortgage life offered by lenders usually has a reducing benefit that runs with the mortgage balance. In other words, as your mortgage balance goes down, the value of your insurance goes down as well, while the premiums remain the same. For example, if you signed a mortgage for $100,000 and there was a claim when the balance was $75,000, the insurance would only cover the remaining balance of $75,000. The surviving spouse would then own the home free-and-clear with the mortgage paid in full.

Some financial experts do not recommend this type of insurance because of its reducing-benefit feature, claiming that term insurance, which we will cover next, pays the full amount insured. In that case, using the same example, the surviving spouse would receive a cheque for $25,000 in addition to the free-and-clear home.

With lender insurance, your premiums, while they will not decline, will also never go up, as long as you do not refinance the mortgage. In the case that you do refinance, or transfer your mortgage to another financial institution, then a new insurance application would be necessary. Since you may very well be older when this event takes place, you could be in for increased premiums.

Term Insurance

Term insurance is just that – insurance for a specific term. Some people take five-year and some ten-year term insurance, sometimes setting it up to coincide with the term of the mortgage. While it's true that term insurance pays a larger benefit than lender insurance, there are some drawbacks:

• **Term insurance premiums are often higher than lender insurance premiums, depending on where you buy it, and what age category you fit in.**
• **When the term runs out, a new application may be necessary and because you are older the premiums will increase.**
• **When the term runs out, a new medical assessment is required, if a physical ailment has developed, your premiums could increase or your application to be insured again could be declined. There is no such risk with lender insurance unless the mortgage is refinanced or transferred. You are covered for life regardless of advancing age or physical condition.**

I usually do not recommend term insurance for these reasons. However, it is always up to the borrower to make the choice.

Reducing Benefit Mortgage Life through Private Insurers

This type of insurance has all the benefits of lender insurance plus the added feature of being portable. In other words, if you decide to refinance your mortgage or transfer it to another institution, you are not forced to re-apply for life-insurance coverage. That's because the insurance is purchased through a private insurance carrier and not the financial institution. So, if you can get a better rate on your mortgage renewal from ABC Bank, you can go for it without having to worry about your insurance premiums climbing. The insurance is there for the life of the mortgage, regardless of where you take it and the premium will never change no matter what changes take place in your medical condition.

To illustrate the effect of having to re-insure on a mortgage transfer, let's consider this. If a forty-five-year-old couple opted for joint life on a lender-insured mortgage of $100,000, their premium would be approximately $39 per month, based on current market rates. If in the following year they transferred to another financial institution, their premium would increase to $56 per month, because they would have entered a new age category. The difference of $17 per month over the remaining twenty-four years of the mortgage would amount to $4,896, if they had the mortgage that long. That's a sizeable difference. If they then transferred again after the sixth year, the premium would climb to $81. The reason? At fifty-one, they would once again be in an entirely new age category requiring markedly higher rates.

This is why the portable mortgage insurance, not tied to the lender, is so valuable. It gives the borrower complete freedom to play the mortgage market without life insurance risk.

If you decide to buy mortgage life from a private insurer, you would do well to have that insurance in place before you attend the mortgage closing. This will help diffuse an all-out attack by the lender, who is duty bound and under threat of dismissal to sell you life insurance. Sometimes lenders will resort to shameful tactics to accomplish their goals, such as implying that the approval for the loan was tied to the purchase of life insurance. I have had many customers over the years tell me about situations such as this. It is my understanding that this type of activity is illegal. Nevertheless, it can be very intimidating to the average consumer, and you need to be aware it could happen to you.

If you announce you have private insurance, the lender may try to challenge it by pointing out their insurance is a few dollars a month cheaper. If you have purchased a quality insurance that gives you the freedom to transfer your mortgage without insurance risk, then the additional premiums may well be worth the investment. Remember, it's the *value* in the product that should determine the price you are willing to pay. If you cave in, cancel your private insurance and take the lender's insurance, you may be compromising your own interests. I recommend you stand firm and trust your own decision.

-13-

How To Keep Your Home

"The more you do of what you're doing, the more you'll get of what you've got."
— Brian Tracy

Once you are a homeowner, there are all kinds of new challenges to face with respect to debt management and that is why there are two chapters devoted to debt in this book. This chapter looks at the challenges the lure of debt poses for homeowners.

You already know that debt management is a vital part of your overall financial plan. Without debt management, most people will likely never be able to set aside the 10 percent of their income necessary for a comfortable retirement because the money simply won't be there. Instead, it will be going out to creditors in the form of minimum monthly payments that will amortize the debt into perpetuity, leaving a mortgage balance still unpaid when the income required to pay it diminishes.

The first thing you must know is that as soon as you become a homeowner you will be deluged with a truckload of credit offers. The banks claim they don't sell their client lists, but soon after you move in to your home you may find offers for "pre-approved" credit cards and lines of credit filling your mailbox. It's as if your newfound homeowner status had been broadcast to the entire credit industry. It's party time as they all compete for your business, business you may not have to give them.

These credit offers cause "The E Factor" in some people to go into overdrive. There is a new sense of well being and security that often comes with the purchase of the first home. Some people, fresh from the largest transaction in which they will ever be involved, suddenly adopt the attitude that they can buy anything they want as long as they can afford the payments.

Lenders such as credit card companies love to extend credit to homeowners instead of renters because they perceive an additional sense of security. Do you know what that security is? They see the client now with an asset that can be seized if something goes wrong, and he or she is unable to pay. That asset is the newly purchased home.

When I was with Friendly Finance, it was company policy to stamp the account record of every customer who was a homeowner. This "Homeowner Stamp" was a signal that any client who visited the branch was to be "solicited" by the counter personnel to borrow more money up to their highest pre-approved credit amount, which was usually shown on the file. The stamp was also used to help identify "targets" for loan solicitation during mail campaigns.

The credit card companies have a goal. They want you to continually carry a balance at or near the spending limit for your entire lifetime, having you pay interest at the highest rate possible. Credit card issuers have stockholders to answer to as well. If not enough of their clients are "maxing out," they send spending inducements in the mail along with the monthly statement. These come in the form of pamphlets advertising products at "bargain" prices, offering them to you only for the asking. Just sign here and send it in. The product will arrive on your doorstep in a few weeks. It's easy. This is the credit card company taking direct aim at "The E Factor" in the consumer with a view toward increasing card balances. These companies know precisely what they are doing and that a certain percentage of the population will buy into their offerings.

Have you received any early evening phone calls from your new credit card company inviting you to make a withdrawal to pay off a competing card balance? They happen all the time and they are geared toward early activation. You may think the credit card company would be offended if you ran your balance up too quickly. On the contrary, they want you maxed out as soon as possible so when the real interest rate kicks in after the "introductory" period, you will be paying a sizeable amount of interest to them every month. For them, it just makes good business sense.

Have you ever opened an envelope containing your monthly credit card statement and wondered how they stuffed all that paper in there? What you are seeing is an attempt by the credit card company to activate your account if you have a zero balance, and to increase your balance if you are already carrying one.

Payments on Payments

This is the most recent "innovation" of the retail industry to increase sales through the extending of credit. They will often divide the total purchase price, minus shipping and taxes, over two, three or even four payments charged to your credit card. In this manner, the entirety of the purchase doesn't hit your card all in one month, and you retain more of your spending limit for other uses. As your credit card statements arrive, and if the balance is not being paid in full, you are effectively making payments on payments. Ridiculous.

It may interest you to know that "credit card activation", as a policy, has been around since the very inception of credit cards in the 1970s. Some of the methods of enticement were very crude compared to today's methods, but were still quite effective. "Activation" letters would be sent out to clients, reminding them of their available credit, and suggesting that they could take a vacation. Join a country club. Within five days of the letter going out, a bank employee would call the customer to make sure they received it, and to add some further enticement to use the card.

For some clients these activation strategies were ineffective; for others, they were moderately effective. But for those most affected by "The E Factor," they were extremely effective, and clients would continue to spend until they were at or over their authorized limits.

When a "maxout" occurred, and the central goal of maximum profit had been achieved, the bank would offer the client a consumer loan to pay off their credit card balances. Thus, credit cards were used as a "feeder product" to help increase consumer loan business.

This rotation of debt from credit cards to loans didn't stop there. With the spending limit freed up, the client would sometimes continue spending, max the card out again and then require another "consolidation loan." Consolidation loans were big business and lenders would often compete against each other for them, sometimes engaging in rate wars. Borrowers would take their consolidated debt from company to company, bank to bank, in search of a more favourable rate and a lower monthly payment.

Consolidation loans would continue until the personal loan was at maximum and the card had to be cancelled. The client had, in fact, enslaved themselves to the lending institution, locked into seemingly never-ending payments. There would sometimes be a flash point where the client would become fed up with the high payments, and resulting lower standard of living, and look for an escape hatch. For some that was bankruptcy. For others, homeowners with equity, this would involve the next stage of consolidation:

Mortgage Refinancing

People would jump at the chance to reduce payments by even a few hundred dollars. Sometimes they would take a second mortgage. Other times, it was necessary to refinance the first mortgage, often with a penalty involved, which only added to the overall cost of borrowing.

Once the new mortgage had "solved" the problem and income had been freed up through reduced payments, some clients would be fine. Others though, would go right back into debt. The entire process would repeat itself until the home equity was completely exhausted, all of it wiped away through financial mismanagement.

I Remember

One of our banking clients applied for a personal loan to consolidate credit card debt. He was massively in debt, owing sizeable amounts on at least a dozen cards. When I pulled his file, I found we had already granted the man a consolidation loan just eight months before and I wondered how he could already be this far into his cards again. Since the man had a proven propensity to incur debt, the lender who granted the last loan cut up all the credit cards and stapled the pieces inside the client's file. In addition, she had sent a letter to each creditor, with the client's authorization, to have the credit lines closed.

When I opened the file the first thing I saw were the destroyed cards. Then I compared them to the debts the man presently owed, and I found he had re-activated every single card that we had closed.

Needless to say, we were not in a position to grant another loan because we knew what the outcome would be.

For many clients bitten with the credit bug there would come a day of reckoning. With the realization that equity was gone and payments were becoming more and more difficult, if not impossible, some people would be inclined to give up and walk away from their homes. They would leave them to the creditors.

It is very possible to lose your home $20 at a time. It is not so much the large purchases but the smaller ones that accumulate over time, that cause the most problems. For some, the end of home equity is the end of the borrowing cycle. However, in the United States, lenders have come up with a new "innovation." For those consumers who have borrowed and spent their equity, but, because of a high income, still have the ability to make higher payments, lenders have introduced "The 125 Loan."

Here, a lender will actually advance 125 percent of your home equity on a first or second mortgage. The market has cast aside common sense in its zeal for profitable loans, lending consumers dollars in excess of their net worth.

In Canada, the banks' interest in granting consolidation loans on an unsecured personal loan basis has abated in recent years. The banks have discovered the wonderful profit potential of the investment market, now making much of their income from stock market transactions. They view this activity as much less risky, and therefore are no longer really interested in unsecured personal loans. They would sooner allow an individual to wallow in their self-induced credit card debt than give them a chance unless, of course, the debtor is willing and able to pledge home equity as security. Then the interest in personal lending is revived.

While it may seem that I'm only blaming the financial institutions, I want to make it clear that I believe they are only partly responsible. In the final analysis, it is the individual who signs on to the credit card, the loan and the mortgage who is ultimately responsible.

Sometimes we have to take a look at the mistakes of others in order to have a sense of the right direction. In that regard, I'm going to share a few examples with you, case histories with relevance to this subject.

The Story of John and Theresa

John and Theresa were approaching fifty. Fifty is an age when the rewards of a lifetime of productive work should begin to appear. Fifty is an age when one should begin to enjoy life more. Fifty is not an age when one wants to be struggling to make ends meet, to be forced to turn on the jets and work even harder.

John and Theresa were indeed approaching fifty but for them the age lacked some of its intended lustre. They had worked very hard for many years, but in the absence of a detailed family budget, they had become locked into a pattern of overspending.

I had occasion to visit this very nice couple at their home one Sunday. They wanted to talk about refinancing a mortgage to repay some debts, a fairly common request these days. When I entered their home I really didn't notice much about it, as I began to engage them in conversation. However, as the conversation progressed, and I began to list their assets and liabilities, I began to take notice of my surroundings.

The following is an overview of John and Theresa's debts:

Creditor	Type of Credit	Limit If Applicable	Balance	Monthly Payment
Bank Loan	Consolidated Credit Cards		$21,000	$705
Bank Loan	Consolidated Credit Cards		$16,000	$425
Leasing Co.	Car Lease		$19,000	$400
Bank	Revolving Line of Credit	$7,500	$7,500	$225
Dept. Store	Card	$4,500	$4,500	$225
Dept. Store	Card	$1,000	$800	$40
Bank	Loan RRSP		$22,000	$220
Bank	Mortgage		$44,000	$395
Totals		$13,000	$134,800	$2,635

By the time I was finished taking this application I was very aware of my surroundings. The house was very sparsely furnished. I had just listed consumer debts in excess of $90,000, and I could't see evidence as to where the money had been spent, except for a newer car that had been leased. The furniture looked as though it had been purchased from a second-hand store. There was nothing in sight that seemed of any real value.

John and Theresa had been heavy spenders all through their youthful years, never really paying much attention to the prospect of retirement. They loved to have fun, and spent their money on things of questionable need and value.

To help you gain a better understanding of their situation, I offer the following summary of points.

• **John and Theresa owed more than $134,000.**
• **Even though they had lived in their home for twenty years, they only had $13,000 in equity. The house should have been paid off by then.**
• **The two bank loans, totalling $37,000, were for consolidation of credit cards.**
• **The banks had since taken the cards away from them leaving them only a line of credit, and a few department store cards.**
• **All of the equity in the home, except the last $13,000, had previously been wiped away by re-mortgaging to clear credit card balances.**
• **All of the existing cards and lines of credit were fully racked up.**
• **The debt ratio vs. income was at maximum, locking John and Theresa into a continuum of minimum monthly payments.**
• **Unless they won the lottery, John and Theresa, at age fifty, had little if any hope of a comfortable retirement.**

John and Theresa had reached the end of their borrowing days. Their situation was so bad I could not find a lender who would even consider helping them.

This is a chilling, if extreme, example of where a lifetime of credit spending can lead. Like John and Theresa, many people in the 80 percent group tend to always be on the wrong side of the ledger – the credit side instead of the asset side. Products are purchased using credit instead of cash from accumulated savings. Moreover, since many people tend to be at their maximum debt vs. income ratio, they are locked into minimum monthly payments and have no money left for saving. When something comes up they have no choice but to turn to credit cards, thus perpetuating the problem.

The fact is you don't have to owe very much money to be off-course in your financial plan. Just that nagging little credit card you've had for years and have never really managed to pay off can represent something much larger than you think.

Let's look at a comparison of the debts of two individuals. The first person maintained an average card balance of $2,500 for twenty-five years and paid the minimum monthly payment of $125. It wasn't a big deal to them. The credit card, and the payment that came with it, was just accepted as a fact of life. Over time, additional purchases, mostly non-essentials, were made as soon as there was enough spending room created to accommodate them.

The second person believed in paying cash whenever possible. Since they didn't maintain a credit card balance, they invested the same $125 per month by paying it to themselves each month instead of to the bank.

With the first scenario at the end of twenty-five years the first person still owed $2,500 and had paid interest charges of over $10,000, while the second person had no credit card balance, and at 8 percent compounded annually, had amassed over $100,000 in savings.

As I said before, if you carry a card balance beyond sixty days, unless there are very unusual circumstances, something is wrong with your financial plan. You had better check it out and correct it. After all, it's one thing for the captain of the ship to be off course for a few hours. But be off course for a few years, and you will wind up in places you never really planned on.

Remember, debt is patient. Debt waits around, testing the outer edges of your financial plan for years, until it finds a weakness, and moves in. Isn't it reassuring, then to know that debt can be conquered? Isn't it heartening to know that the purveyors of debt can be identified, their plans exposed and their efforts defeated?

Purveyors of Debt

It is not my intention to demonize the retail industry. They work very hard in an extremely competitive environment. But in order to resist needless purchases, it may be necessary to look at anyone selling a product or service in a different light, in your own mind. Consider, for your own purposes, that debt is your mortal enemy and the retailer the distributor of that debt. Perhaps then, debt avoidance will become easier.

Credit Card Issuers

We've already taken a look at credit cards, both in the first chapter on debt and in this one. However, since some of the card issuers are becoming more aggressive and their marketing techniques more cunning, perhaps it's worthwhile to take one last look at some of these programs.

The credit card solicitations you receive in the mail, on average, have certain key elements in common. They may include:

• **An unbelievably low interest rate, good for about three to six months. Then the rate skyrockets.**
• **A statement that the offer is time-limited. One of the oldest tricks in the book to get people to "buy now." Why do they use it? It works!**
• **A statement or impression made about status. Yes, a platinum card can be a status symbol when plunked down at a luncheon meeting. It goes well with the financed Rolex watch it exposes.**
• **A claim that you have been pre-approved.**
• **An offer for life insurance coverage. Since they know you will always have a balance, the card companies seek to protect themselves by offering credit life insurance coverage. They also get a piece of the action from the insurance company for selling the coverage.**
• **A claim that you were specifically selected for this program. It's "by invitation only." (Your name was in the phone book.)**
• **Mention of an unbelievably large credit line only Donald Trump could qualify for. Your limit is $1,500.**
• **A promise of "benefits" like collision coverage, roadside assistance and one of the most popular of all, accidental death and dismemberment insurance, another profit vehicle for the credit card issuer.**
• **Mention of the absence of an annual fee. This is**

described as "savings."
• A 25-day interest-free grace period from interest charges on purchases. The credit card company charges the merchants for this. The merchants charge you.

I have seen people receive an average of one of these offers a week through the mail soon after they bought a home. Many win approval for more cards, even though their ability to pay them all has not been established. On the other hand, I have also seen people apply for credit multiple times, with limited, if any success. The company requests a credit file on each application, even though they say the client is "pre-approved." The large number of inquiries this places on the credit report also tends to drive down the credit score.

I once met a man who had twenty-five inquiries on his credit report within a six-month period, all from the same department store. He said every time he went into the store someone would be standing there asking him to fill out a credit application. They turned him down every time but he kept applying anyway. It was practically impossible to get him a mortgage because the lenders were able to see all of his failed attempts at applying for that one lousy card.

Finance Companies

Some people like to finance purchases through a store's private label financing program over three, six or twelve months on an interest-free basis. The merchant then sells your sales contract or sales slip to finance companies. When the finance company buys your sales contract, the merchant is paid in full and does not carry any credit account on your behalf.

Just as banks used their credit card portfolios as a "feeding device" for their consumer loan business, so too do finance companies. In fact, sourcing their business from retail merchants brings in 95 percent of all the business that finance companies receive. They just don't get people walking in for Christmas loans like they used to.

As their market share has eroded over the years, finance companies have had to become increasingly more aggressive in their marketing campaigns to survive. As a result they adopted various forms of mailers which were like instant credit vehicles that really get "The E Factor" hopping. Enter the credit voucher.

If you have a finance company account originated through a store, and you are a homeowner, you can rest assured you will be receiving credit vouchers on a regular basis – enough perhaps to wallpaper the family room. These vouchers are usually pre-approved – truly pre-approved – and only require your signature to be exchanged for hard cash. They are easy to negotiate and the rates range commonly from 24 percent to 33 percent, whatever the market will bear. They appeal to the truly desperate credit seeker who has exhausted or maxed out all other sources.

Automobile Dealer

Paid cash for any car you've bought in the last twenty years? This practice, common in the years of the Model T, seems to have come to an abrupt end. Now, we don't want to trash the automobile dealers too much. They are out to make a living just like the rest of us. Nevertheless, they are purveyors of debt in the sense that most people have to finance cars in order to afford them. The dealers sometimes push credit, even more than the virtues of their products, in order to sell vehicles. They know this strategy works. It all boils down to the monthly payment. How low can we get it? The payment and not the price determines whether most consumers will take the deal. Never mind what's behind the monthly payment.

Zero interest. Zero down. Low monthly payments. Three months worth of "free" gas. It's easy. C'mon down! Who can blame the dealers for using these methods given the ridiculous prices of cars these days?

It's not such a bad thing to drive a new car. In fact it can be a real kick. Question is, can you afford it and keep your financial plan on course? If you can, buy the darn thing! After all, life is to be enjoyed. However, if the purchase will throw you off course, you had better think twice. Perhaps old Betsy could do with a new set of brakes, or even a valve job to help keep your financial ship afloat. The old girl will still get you from point A to point B, and you will breathe easier with the absence of debt as you watch your friends choking on their $450 per month lease payments.

I want to briefly discuss one more credit vehicle with particularly insidious consequences. This one is responsible for helping people delay the payoff of their mortgage so far into the future they often cannot manage to live long enough to experience mortgage freedom day. This purveyor may be the most insidious of them all.

The Secured Line of Credit

This one comes under various fancy names depending on the financial institution. They've all done their homework in making it look like a wonderful idea. Essentially, the secured line of credit has a pre-set spending limit, a big one, registered as either a first or second mortgage on your house. You can usually borrow up to 75 percent of the appraised value, less any existing mortgages if you can prove you can make the payments. Instead of accessing your credit line with a credit card, you do it with a personal cheque or a withdrawal. Usually the rates are very attractive, often offered at prime for select borrowers.

For all but the most sophisticated borrowers, a secured line of credit is a time bomb in the hands of the average consumer, set to explode and blow the roof right off your financial plan and your home.

I used to work for a company that conducted most of its consumer lending in open-ended revolving lines of credit, both secured and unsecured. We had a large portfolio of secured lines of credit. Some were based on 3 percent repayment of the balance monthly, and on some we accepted interest only, allowing the borrower to decide when to repay principal.

Would it surprise you to learn that the vast majority of these secured lines of credit operated at or near the maximum limit all the time? People were making ill-advised consumer purchases, mostly toys and non-essentials, with their home equity. How sad.

If you are an average consumer with a bit of a weakness when it comes to credit and you want to make sure your mortgage is never paid off, if you want to virtually assure yourself a lifetime of mortgage payments, by all means, sign up for a secured line of credit! Otherwise, take my advice and never risk your financial future by writing cheques against your equity.

Insurance Coverage

Premiums for life and disability insurance on debt only add to the already spiralling cost of borrowing. Credit card issuers are now engaged in selling additional types of insurance coverage, such as accidental death and dismemberment.

The credit card insurance business has become big business with more and more card issuers making arrangements with various insurance carriers. Remember, there is usually a premium paid to the credit card issuer by the insurance company for selling their products, and this premium is added onto the cost of the insurance. The result is that you pay to help support all of the profit earners in the chain, and the insurance is therefore probably more expensive than insurance you could buy from your local independent agent.

The marketing of these insurance products is done daily, and nightly. You may receive a call about it at dinnertime, right after the call from the local telephone company who is crying about the fact you switched your long-distance service.

The telemarketers will use all means within legal limits to get you to say yes and the most common is the thirty-day free trial. You take the insurance, look it over for thirty days and the credit card company will foot the bill for the first few month's premiums. You can cancel if you decide you don't like the insurance. The insurance sellers are using a theory that says that a certain percentage of people who take the insurance coverage will retain it.

All things considered, there are monumental benefits that will come your way if you can manage to stay out of debt. Paying off high interest credit cards is a way of earning returns you could not match in any other type of investment, and there's no element of risk. If you have a credit card balance of $2,500 at 18 percent, paying it off yields a risk-free 18 percent return on your money. It's called investing in your debt, investing in yourself and investing in your future.

-14-

How To Successfully Buy Your Next Home

"Dreading the climax of all human ills
The inflammation of his weekly bills."
— Lord Byron, Don Juan.

The average next home buyer makes crucial mistakes in this process which can cumulatively destroy their plans for retirement. I realize that's a fairly strong statement, but it's true. I have seen more examples of it over the years than I care to think about.

The first glaring error most next home buyers make is that they go right back to their current lender, accepting whatever deal is offered, and fail to check that offer against the market.

The failure to shop for a mortgage on the next home purchase can have consequences that are just as devastating as they are on the first home purchase, perhaps even more so. So why don't people shop? Let's look at some possible reasons:

- **Misguided loyalty to the financial institution.**
- **Fear of change.**
- **Fear that they'll be rejected by another lender because they are not known by that lender. They fail to realize the new lender would likely roll out the red carpet for them.**
- **Penalties. The current lender may be using the threat of penalties as a financial club to scare them into remaining with that lender.**

Let's examine the penalty question, as we have already discussed the other factors earlier. Say you visit your lender one day to announce you're going to buy your next home and you will be shopping around for a mortgage this time. You're checking with your lender first.

Guaranteed, if you are talking to a negative-power lender, they will haul out the penalty club and hit you right over the head with it, without hesitation. Please do not allow yourself to be intimidated by a lender dealing with you in this negative manner. Ask them "What can you do for me that your competition cannot?"

This question will likely place the lender in presentation mode, and neutralize some of the power they *think* they have over you. In reality, they have no power over you at all. Remember, as the consumer, you are the one with the real power.

The lender should begin to offer positive reasons why you should choose their services once again. The lenders do not *deserve* your business. They must earn it every time.

You may indeed be faced with a penalty on your mortgage of either three months interest or interest differential, if the market rates are now lower for the remaining term than your present rate. An interest differential penalty cannot be charged if your mortgage is mortgage-default insured, and is beyond its third anniversary. In that case, the lender must only charge three months interest.

The lender may offer to blend the penalty into the new rate you are being offered so you don't have to pay it out of pocket. Most people will jump at the chance to avoid a lump-sum expenditure, another temptation caused by "The E Factor." However, blending the penalty increases the cost of borrowing, as you are financing the penalty over the term of the mortgage. It's always cheaper to pay a penalty, if you have the means to do so, than it is to blend it.

So, why not shop around? If the threat of penalty is the only thing the lender can think of to keep you, then that's a sign in itself you should be going elsewhere. Remember, there is more to a mortgage than just the rate or the penalty. Other features we have discussed like flexible prepayment allowances also play a role and may have a more substantial affect on the overall cost of borrowing than the rate or penalty itself.

There are thousands of possible scenarios, too numerous to address within these pages. However in shopping around I hope you will encounter at least one purebred lending professional who will be able to advise you on the merits of blending versus switching in your own specific situation.

One of the hazards of blending is that the lender can build in a signifigant profit without you knowing about it. Unless you have taken courses in finance, you will not likely be able to quantify those profits. In addition to a penalty, the "add rate" (the rate at which the lender calculates the additional amount you are borrowing) could be at the full posted rate as opposed to a discounted rate. Some lenders may recognize your loyalty or unwillingness to shop around and use that as an opportunity to build as much profit into the blended rate as possible.

For example, let's say you have one year left on your term at 6.5 percent and rates have gone up to 7.5 percent. You need to borrow additional funds to accommodate your next purchase so the lender offers to let you keep your 6.5 percent on the existing mortgage balance and charge you 7.5 percent on the additional amount you want to borrow, blending the two rates and possibly extending the term.

At this point, consumers often fail to realize that the add rate can also be negotiated. Who says you have to pay posted rate on the add portion? It is just as negotiable as a rate would be on a brand new mortgage. If you can bring the add rate down, it will bring down the overall blended rate. Make sense? The impact of the reduced add rate on the overall blended rate will depend on the size of the additional amount you are borrowing in relation to your current balance.

If you find this confusing, don't worry, most people do. Just remember, all this haggling over rate and penalty is nickel-and-dime stuff compared to the impact of amortization on the cost of borrowing. Most people get so caught up in the rate game they forget about the amortization, and jack it right back up to twenty-five years, obliterating any savings they may have negotiated on the rate anyway.

I have one more bit of advice to offer on blending. If, after shopping the market thoroughly, you decide that blending is definitely for you, you may find it comforting to know you don't necessarily have to do it with your existing lender.

If you want to take your business elsewhere, another lender may be willing to blend the penalty for you. It's something being touted as new to the market, but in actual fact it is just the age-old practice of mortgage discounting in disguise. The new lender will charge you a premium on top of the lowest rate you can negotiate, and that rate premium will represent the equivalent of the penalty you owe to the other lender. The new lender will then just cut a cheque for the amount of your penalty and pay your former lender. Voila! You will have just changed lenders without having to dig into your pockets to pay a lump sum penalty.

Given the competitive nature of the mortgage market, you are never really locked into anything. Don't view your existing mortgage situation as a form of financial paralysis. Shop around. You will be amazed at the deals you can get!

Let's move on. A local real-estate agent told me recently that she was having a difficult time finding financing for next home buyers. I was quite taken aback by this statement, and since I'm in the business of helping people obtain mortgage financing, I was interested in what she had to say.

I already knew from past experience that some next home buyers would have trouble because they fail to execute a financial plan after purchasing their first homes. Nevertheless, I did not know or realize that the problems that buyers were having qualifying for their next homes had reached the point that realtors were starting to notice it as a developing trend. I asked the realtor what it was specifically that was causing these problems. Care to guess what she said?

Debt.

Just the topic we finished discussing in the last chapter! I am willing to bet it will not come as a surprise to you that the two major debt factors which absolutely destroy the plans of consumers to buy the next home are . . .

Credit cards and car payments.

In the case of credit cards, the purchasing of trinkets, gadgets and other items of questionable necessity will in time lead to staggering credit card balances that cause the applicant to fail the affordability test. If that isn't bad enough, the decision to buy that new car on the never-never plan at $450 per month will only make the financial situation worse and dash the applicant's next home aspirations.

The great wonder of all this is that these same homeowners, weighed down by debt, are oblivious to the fact that there is no way they could possibly afford a larger mortgage payment. Many of them go out shopping for homes and write offers without even attempting to be pre-approved by their bankers! In fact, some people actually enter into a contract to sell their existing homes without first being approved for the next mortgage and are then declined for that mortgage. The result? Renting once again!

All this might seem unbelievable to you. How could someone mess up so badly that they borrow themselves right out of their homes? How could someone accept an offer to sell their home with no dreaming idea if they will be able to secure a mortgage for the next one?

However, you would be surprised (or maybe not, by now) to know how easy it is to get caught in a very unfortunate situation when you're trying to buy the next home! It has to be done carefully to be successful. We are going to discuss how, and show you what happens when details are overlooked.

The Story of George and Mary

George and Mary had purchased their home four years ago. At that time, they had had just one child. Now with three children, they had outgrown their small bungalow and were looking to buy a larger home in a better neighbourhood. Their eldest child was coming of school age and they wanted to find the best possible environment for their children to grow up in.

At the time that George and Mary had bought their first home, they had qualified with very little difficulty. The following is an overview of their financial situation just after their first home purchase:

George & Mary

Total Monthly Income	$4,100.00
Purchase Price of Home	$95,000.00
Mortgage & Mortgage-Default Premiums	$93,634.00
Monthly Payments, Taxes and Heat	$930.83
Payments as Percent of Income	
(GDS) (32% maximum)	22.68%
Credit Cards ($3,400 total)	$170.00
Total Payments	$1,100.83

Percent of Monthly Income
(TDS) (40% maximum)   26.83%
Vehicles owned: 1988 Tempo (paid off)
                    1991 Grand Am (paid off)

Before George and Mary bought this home, and for the first three years of their marriage, they had been renting. Even though they had started out debt-free, with furniture and other essentials given to them by their families, they had always found it difficult to save. It had always seemed like there was never anything left out of each paycheque. They each had had a credit card, and they had used the cards to purchase things they needed for their apartment.

This financial snapshot of George and Mary is fairly typical for the average to above-average first home buyer. Some first-time buyers enter the mortgage market with more debt than George and Mary. So, in that respect, they had done a comparatively good job at maintaining their debts well within affordability standards. Even so, they had not realized the necessity of paying oneself first, and as a consequence, they had no savings. They were forced to approach family for the down payment.

They had made little financial progress over the years, and so were going to rely on the profit they would make from the sale of the first home to cover the down payment they would need for the next.

They calculated, based on the appraisal of their realtor, that their home was now worth $110,000. After real-estate fees and other expenses they thought that they should be able to clear $102,000. Mortgage interest rates had gone up, then down, and were now exactly at 7 percent, the same George and Mary had originally borrowed. The bank agreed to waive the penalty, and since their mortgage balance was now approximately $87,000, they would have $15,000 towards their down payment and closing costs for the next purchase.

The couple had been driving around looking at homes and had decided that the $135,000 price range would be best. This way they could put 10 percent down, $13,500, and have $1,500 left for legal fees. If that wasn't enough, they would take another $1,000 from savings, which had managed to accumulate since the last purchase.

George and Mary were now ecstatic over the idea of a better home for their family, and they made an appointment at the bank to apply for a pre-approved mortgage. The following chart shows how their application now looked to their banker, four years after their first home purchase:

George & Mary

Total Family Monthly Income	$4,500.00
Purchase Price of New Home	$135,000.00
Mortgage & Default-insurance Premiums (After 10% Down)	$124,537.00
Payments, Including Taxes and Heat @7% APR	$1,197.28
Payments as Percentage of Income (GDS) (32% maximum)	26.60%
Monthly Payments on Credit Cards	$375.00
New Car Payment	$425.00
Total Payments	$1,997.00
Percentage of Monthly Income (TDS) (40% maximum)	44.38%
Vehicles owned: 1991 Grand Am (paid off) 1998 4 X 4 (Leased)	

Here is an overview of George and Mary's application as seen through they eyes of the banker.

> • **George had received a few raises over the years, and the total family income had increased from $4,100 to $4,500 per month. Even so, they had not been doing a good job at saving, having only $1,000 in the bank.**
> • **Their credit card balances had ballooned from $3,400 to $7,000 in just four years, indicating they were spending more than they were making with the overflow being charged to the cards.**
> • **They had leased a new vehicle with a high monthly payment.**
> • **The financial strain of the added obligations was beginning to show up on the credit reports of both George and Mary, as they were now occasionally late with their payments. It wasn't serious yet, but there were definitely some cracks in their financial plan, if**

they had one at all.

• Their affordability ratios were now outside of guidelines with respect to the total debt ratio (TDS). They could still afford the home based on the first test (GDS), but the additional borrowings had acted to impair their ability to pay a higher mortgage payment.

"You can't afford this," the lender said.

"What?" Mary exclaimed.

"I'm sorry, your mortgage application does not meet our underwriting guidelines, and we are therefore unable to help you this time."

George and Mary looked at each other in disbelief. George tried to gather himself. "Why? What's wrong here?" he asked.

"Well, you have increased your debt payments substantially. Your credit card balances have doubled since you bought your first home and then the new vehicle lease really drove your affordability ratio over the limit."

Mary's 1988 Tempo had been breaking down more frequently and the repairs had been straining their budget. Then George saw a great deal one day at the local dealer. He could get a new vehicle on a two-year lease with zero down. He discussed it with Mary and they went for the deal. It was much easier to them than spending $1,000 they didn't have on transmission repairs for the Tempo. Besides, how long would it last?

Now, George was thinking about that day at the dealership. He hadn't planned to buy a new vehicle. He was actually on his way to the transmission shop to get an estimate for repairs on the Tempo, when he saw the sign above the dealer's lot advertising the 4 x 4. Considering the news he was now hearing from the banker, the idea of transmission repairs was looking much better to George. But it was too late. George re-entered the conversation.

"Isn't there anything you can do for us? We really need a larger home."

"I'm sorry," said the banker.

"Can you consolidate our credit card debt and reduce the payments?" Mary asked.

"Well, no. You see, the payment reduction would not be enough to qualify. In addition, your credit score is too low because of your recent borrowing activity, and some of your payments have been late. Your car, the 1991 Grand Am, is not worth the $7,000 required to secure the loan."

George and Mary knew that. They finally realized the extent of the struggle they were having meeting their obligations. Things had been going reasonably well until they bought the 4 x 4. They were making the payments, but as always, they were unable to save because of debt.

"How do you see this turning out for us?" asked George. "I can't sell a vehicle I don't own, and I have eighteen months to go on the lease."

"Well, obviously you need to get rid of that payment but it's not your only problem. You need to sit down and make a budget for yourselves so that you don't overspend. In the next eighteen months you can turn in the vehicle, perhaps buy an inexpensive used car and then work on reducing your credit card debt. I would say if you follow a plan like that you should be able to re-apply successfully within two years."

George was listening to all of this while holding his head in his hands. "If only I had fixed that damn car instead of leasing the truck."

The negative consequences of failing to have a financial plan had now come into clear view for George and Mary. In fact, they had never really planned anything. The first house was a spur-of-the-moment decision for which they were financially unprepared. The truck was an impulse buy, made to look like an easier purchase by the dealer than it actually was. Their numerous credit card purchases could not have been that important since they couldn't remember more than a half-dozen items they had purchased totaling $1,200. The $7,000 balance was a mystery.

As stunning as all of this news was for George and Mary, they were going to be okay. They still had their home, for which they were suddenly finding a new appreciation. And, they were going to bite the bullet, weed out all of the unnecessary expenses from their budget, pay down their credit cards and get rid of the truck as soon as the lease term was up. Then, they would find an old car in good repair and reapply for their next dream home, the one in which they would eventually retire.

George and Mary had learned a valuable lesson. They vowed never to take financial action without planning again.

This is a very typical story these days. Homeowners are finding the doors to the next home locked when they try the keys. I don't know what the failure rate is, but it is certainly high enough to have people in the industry talking about it. It all stems from a lack of planning and a propensity to make purchases on credit, which represent wants rather than needs. There is nothing wrong with serving a want if you can afford it. But if it is going to blow a hole in your budget, hold off! Worse yet, if you make the purchase and subsequently realize it was beyond your affordability... well, it's tough getting the toothpaste back in the tube!

Now, you may have found this story a bit frustrating. Yet, frustrating is a few shades better than devastating. For all that George and Mary did wrong, they did something else very right. Do you know what it is? George and Mary decided to apply for mortgage pre-approval *before* they sold their home!

For reasons I don't understand, some homeowners enter into a contract to sell their homes without first being approved for the next purchase. When they do finally wander into the bank to apply for a mortgage, they are very often greeted with a cold slap in the face. How do you think the story of George and Mary would have ended had they sold their home first? Unhappily at best, for them and for their children. The very idea of selling the current home without a fully approved next purchase lined up, complete with financing, is so misguided I find it difficult finding words to describe it. But it does happen.

I had the unhappy experience of being directly involved in a situation just like this recently. I was approached by a man who was having trouble obtaining financing for a next home purchase. His credit rating had deteriorated somewhat since his initial home purchase, his debt had increased and he had opened his own business, all in the last few years. I tried everything I could and no lender wanted to touch him. The man had sold his home just the week before he decided to start looking for the mortgage.

The road to the next home is fraught with danger for a majority of the current homeowner population. But this road can still be travelled, if it is done carefully. Things must be done in the right order. Otherwise, the results can be extremely unpleasant.

As a lender, I have seen many ways in which the financial condition of an aspiring borrower can deteriorate to the point to where the borrower would no longer qualify for a mortgage.

We've discussed the effects of credit changes. There are others. Some of the more common ones pertain to changes in the workplace. Since these can have significant effects, I thought I would share a few of them with you:

Job Change

Whether you are planning a job change or one comes unexpectedly along, you should know that the job change, while it may be a step in the right career direction, may be used against you when you apply for credit.

If you have less than 25 percent down, you will require mortgage-default insurance to protect the lender. The insurers will usually require you to have spent one year in your present job, unless you can show a continuous work history *in the same occupation* for more than one year. In the absence of this, you may be declined for a mortgage even if your affordability is well within the guidelines.

While you may be approved by some lenders if you can demonstrate the continuous work history under the insurance guidelines, others will stick to their guns demanding one year on the present job. These lenders may blame the insurance companies in order to transfer responsibility. Don't be fooled by this mumbo jumbo. If you are uncertain about it, call the insurer yourself. They have some very helpful people who can quickly tell you if what you are hearing from the lender is true.

Change of Job Status

In the new global economy, change in job status is not uncommon. If a wage earner in your family has undergone a change from full time to anything else, it may affect your financial plan as well as your lender's view of your application.

Mortgage applicants who work part time are often called upon to prove their income over a three-year period with income tax documentation. Lenders may use a three-year average of income for the affordability test. If the part-time income has not been regular, the income from one or more of the three years could act to pull down the average below the threshold of affordability.

In most cases, if the part-time income is regular, and can be supported through a letter from the employer, you should be fine. But beware of lenders who may be looking for more documentation than you are able to provide.

If the part-time income is derived from casual employment, it may not be counted at all, and should not be relied upon to service a mortgage unless it has proven to be reliable.

Employment by Contract

These days more and more people are employed under contract. This makes lenders nervous. Even though someone gainfully employed and not under contract could be fired in a minute, contract employment will be seen by some lenders as a dead-end temporary position. There are a wide variety of contract employment arrangements in the marketplace, too numerous to list here. Some of them are very financially rewarding, contrary to the negative view of lenders. Even so, every contract arrangement will be looked at on a case-by-case basis and it may be tough to find a lender to sign on. If they do, they may require a three-year track record of continuous employment as evidence your contract has been renewed at least once, together with income documentation from Revenue Canada.

Newly Self Employed

If you are newly self employed you may have to wait three years to buy a home unless you can find someone with the financial strength to back you as a guarantor or co-applicant on title.

New businesses must be proven to be sufficiently income producing before lenders will show any interest. This usually applies no matter how large your down payment. However, there are some lenders called "equity lenders" which would agree to financing before the three years if you have 50 percent down.

Mortgage Default Insurance in Canada

Mortgage default insurance it is of extreme importance to anyone who is purchasing a home with less than 25 percent down. Now, it used to be that the insuring process consisted of two separate and distinct parts – qualification of the borrower and qualification of the property.

Most lenders were entrusted by insurers to qualify the borrowers

with respect to ability and intent to repay. The lenders would ana-
lyze the credit report, perform the affordability test and make sure
the income was reliable enough to service the mortgage payments.
This process is called "credit underwriting." Only in rare cases
would insurers become involved directly. If default later occurred,
the insurance company would examine the file. If the lender had not
done their job according to standards, they could have to forfeit
their claim or have it reduced. The insurance company would
directly take part in qualifying the property by examining the
appraisal and perhaps even doing one itself.

In my experience this system always seemed to work well. But
the insurers, in assessing losses they had taken, came to the conclusion that the borrower was more important than the property
itself in a mortgage transaction. In fact, they came to the conclusion that their lack of direct involvement in the underwriting
process was the reason for spiralling losses. This conclusion, if
valid, was a condemnation of the job the financial institutions had
been doing in qualifying borrowers.

Today, insurance companies are playing a more active role in
the underwriting process. Using advancements in technology, they
are now inspecting the credit reports of mortgage applicants,
examining employment conditions and, in some cases, they are
reversing decisions made by the lenders to grant mortgages.

What does this mean for the average consumer? It means the
pre-approval certificate you received from your bank may be even
more meaningless than you thought! Your banker may be genuinely in favour of approving your mortgage application, yet when
they apply for insurance coverage, they could be rejected because
someone working for the insurer doesn't like your credit report or
your employment situation or both. They may also take exception
to a gifted down payment for some applications even though the
rules say gifts are acceptable. This means the insurance company
is second-guessing the lender and it puts the consumer, unaware of
these developments, at extreme risk.

Let's suppose a well-meaning homeowner wanted to upgrade.
They didn't want to make an offer on the next property without
knowing their current home could be sold for the price they wanted. So they approached the bank and obtained a pre-approval certificate. They may also have been so diligent as to bring their job
letters and proof of down payment so that the only remaining con-

ditions on the certificate would be sale of their current home and default insurance.

In years gone by, homeowners could then go forward with confidence, sell their homes and then finalize the purchase of another. I suppose the order in which one wanted to do this was a matter of personal consideration. Some people would want to make an offer subject to the sale first.

However, either way it's done in today's environment, the home seller is still being exposed to substantial risk if the insurance company eventually decides to decline the purchase after the sale has been completed. That is, unless the home seller has taken the precaution of writing an offer subject to the sale and having the purchase approved right through to the final stage, including insurance, before a commitment is made to sell the current property. Only in this way can anyone be confident they will still be homeowners after this process is all over.

Seller Beware

Of course, the drawback to doing things this way is your pending offer could be bumped while you are waiting for your home to sell. Thus, unless you decide to take the gamble and remove your conditions, you lose the house you just bought and the whole process starts over again. Many people find it particularly demoralizing and discouraging to lose a home on a pending offer. It is certainly a hassle to keep going through this process time and time again, especially if your current home takes longer to sell. However, compared to the risks for most next home buyers, it may be the only sensible course. All of this because the the lenders *and* insurance companies have to agree on the merits of your mortgage application.

For those who do not require mortgage-default insurance (those who offer a down payment of more than 25 percent), selling first may still be a gamble. Always get approval from your lender in writing first. Remember, if you are selling your home and require financing for the next, *always* get final approval from your lender and from the insurer (if required) in writing for the next purchase *before* you sell your current home. The lender approval should consist of:

• **A letter from the lender detailing the amount, rate and terms of the mortgage together with mention of the rate-guarantee period.**
• **A statement in the lender's letter that all conditions, including default insurance, have been satisfied.**
• **A copy of the default insurance certificate, if available.**

There are other things you must consider when making the decision to buy your next home. Certainly the primary consideration should be whether a next home purchase fits into your financial plan.

We know that a properly structured mortgage is the cornerstone of any wealth creation strategy. According to your financial plan, at what age have you targeted mortgage freedom? Do you know the vast majority of next home buyers don't bother to make this consideration? That may be because most people in the bottom 80 percent group do not have a financial plan beginning in the early years of their working lives. Some don't start until they are in their forties and fifties, perhaps at a time when a comfortable retirement has become a mathematical impossibility and continued employment has begun to look less certain.

We can't change the years gone by. That's why it's so important to make the right decisions when they come along. With respect to the next home purchase, there's a fairly easy way to determine affordability, and the fit this purchase may have with your plans.

Say you purchased your first home at age thirty and you had a financial plan to become mortgage free by age fifty. You were absolutely committed to the idea of it because you and your spouse planned to significantly increase your monthly investment allocation by that time. In fact, you had realized the re-investment value of mortgage payments paid to yourself instead of the bank could be truly significant and you were looking forward to increasing the value of your nest egg in time for a planned retirement at age sixty-five.

Now at age thirty-nine, you both decide, for whatever reason, that you want to move into a better home. This will be the last home purchase you plan - the home you want to retire in. Perfect.

Here is where the decisions you made in setting up your mortgage nine years ago can really help you or hinder you. The following table shows a comparison between the way most people would have set up their mortgages and the way you did. We'll call the other people the Joneses, the very people some of us are always trying to keep up with!

Factors	The Joneses Mortgage With a 75bps Rate Discount to Lower Payments	Your Mortgage With A 75bps Discount Applied to Reduce Amortization
Mortgage Amount	$95,000.00	$95,000.00
Rate	7%	7%
Amortization	25 years	17.95 years
Payments	$665.39 monthly	$354.98 bi-weekly
Balance at age 39	$77,232.76	$61,586.70

As you can see, you are miles ahead of the other borrower in the race for mortgage freedom, a very nice advantage when looking to buy the next home. Why? You owe less, so you have more equity to invest in the next purchase. *Therefore, you won't have to borrow as much to complete that purchase!*

Now, let's develop this chart more fully:

Factors	The Joneses Mortgage With a 75bps Rate Discount to Lower Payments	Your Mortgage With a 75bps Discount Applied to Reduce Amortization
Mortgage Amount	$95,000.00	$95,000.00
Rate	7%	7%
Amortization	25 years	17.95 years
Payments	$665.39 monthly	$354.98 bi-weekly
Balance at age 39	$77,232.76	$61,586.70
Remaining Amortization	16 years	8.95 years
Price of Current Home	$120,000.00	$120,000.00

Equity for Next Purchase after Expenses of 7%	$34,367.24	$50,013.30
Next Home Purchase	$165,000.00	$165,000.00
Mortgage Required (Approx.)	$133,212.00	$115,000.00
Rate	7%	7%
Amortization	25 years	11 years
Payments	$933.04 + $235.00 taxes & heat monthly = $1168.00	$622.83 bi-weekly + $235.00 taxes & heat monthly
Family Monthly Income	$5,900.00	$5,900.00
Affordability Test #1 (GDS)	19.80%	26.85%
Debt Payments (car $450, $200 loan, $300 credit cards)	$950.00	0
Total Payments	$2,118	$1,584.47 monthly equivalent, heat excl.
Affordability Test # 2 (TDS)	35.90%	26.85%
Target Age for Mortgage freedom	64	50
Reinvestment cost of Mortgage Payments Until Retirement, $1,350 a month @ 8%, compounded annually	0	$500,000 (Approx.)

For comparison sake, we have assumed all mortgages are fully amortized.

This is now a fairly substantial chart, and as you can see, there is a significant difference in the bottom line. So let's look at a brief analysis in point form to see how you won the day over the Joneses.

- The Joneses made their first mistake when they negotiated the mortgage on their first home. They set the amortization at the maximum, and used their rate discount to lower the payments as much as possible. They had plans for some purchases.
- You did it right. You understood the value of converting a rate discount to reduced amortization. Your decision to take accelerated bi-weekly payments meant that your remaining amortization was even lower than you had planned on by age thirty-nine. So, you were comfortable with setting it at 11 years because it still conformed to your financial plan calling for mortgage freedom by age fifty.
- The Joneses amortized the next purchase over 25 years all over again. They had to if the purchase was to fall into their affordability range. Over the years the Joneses had never found it possible to save. When they needed something they often paid for it with a credit card, on which they usually paid the minimum payment. They had to. They always seemed to have a new vehicle and were stretching to make the payments. Without a financial plan, they never really kept track of their finances and didn't realize the car payments were causing a deficit in their monthly budget, which was spilling onto their cards. The cards had ballooned into a debt of $6,000 once again, after a credit card consolidation loan just two years prior.
- You did it right. You were able to keep your financial plan on target. You paid off your credit cards monthly for the most part, only carrying balances over sixty days a few times. You paid yourself first, bought the things you needed out of accumulated savings and, thanks to a little discipline, you were able to buy a newer vehicle every five years or so with cash or a short-term loan.
- The Joneses came to the end of the trail penniless, except for about $20,000 equity in their home. Because of their continuing habits of credit spending, they had

refinanced their mortgage twice over the years and added a second mortgage through a finance company at a high rate of interest to consolidate debts.

• **You did it right.** By age forty-nine, with the advantage of accelerated bi-weekly payments, you were mortgage free. You then began to make your mortgage payments to yourself instead of the bank. At approximately $1,350 per month, you amassed a sizable fortune. By age sixty-five you had a free-and-clear home and more than $500,000 to add to the retirement nest egg you had been building over the years.

Just imagine the choices the Joneses were faced with in retirement. Their home would have to be sold, as they were no longer able to make the payments. With only pension income to fall back on, they would look back on all the years of excess spending, bearing the pain of regret.

On the other hand, the comparatively minor pain of the discipline you exercised over the years paid off for you substantially! You had many more choices, happier ones to be faced with. Your retirement nest egg could now be paid back to you monthly to complement your pension income and provide a comfortable, worry-free existence. You could even afford to travel more than during your working years. You could sell that big home and buy a condo. You now hate yard work! It interferes with all of your activities.

The possibilities are all but endless for those who make the right decisions. The differences between you and the Joneses were very small to start out with, but they accumulated into great ones over time. That's the value of financial planning. *The tiny disciplines were worth $500,000 dollars!*

-15-

How To Manage Your Mortgage

"There is a gigantic difference between earning a great deal of money and being rich."
                                        — Marlene Dietrich.

Mortgage management,through the reduction of borrowing costs, is key to increased savings. Even if you have signed on to a closed term mortgage, such as a five-year, you could make significant financial gains by simply managing your mortgage.

The degree to which you can save is partially determined by how well you watch the mortgage market. Of course, we know that those who opt for variable rate mortgages are market watchers to begin with. However, your closed mortgage should carry the right for the borrower to early renew if there is a change in rates to your benefit. If this right does not appear in the contract, the financial institution may have a side policy for early renewals. Most lenders today will allow early renewal whether it's in the contract or not in order to remain competitive in an increasingly challenging environment.

If rates have come down since you last set up your mortgage, and the reduction in rate is enough to cover the penalty you incur, with additional savings beyond that, then it might make sense to early renew. You know what the rates are today, but you don't know what the rates will be tomorrow. So the strategy some people take is to early renew at a time they believe the mortgage market has bottomed out. They then extend the term back to the original five years, or longer, as an extra insurance policy against a volatile interest rate market down the road.

Several years ago, rates came down from 11 percent to around

8.5 percent for a five-year term. I can remember processing several early renewals during that period. At the same time, the major trust company down the street maintained a policy of not allowing early renewal. Customers applying for the lower rates were being turned away. This trust company was very friendly with what I call "the front end" of the mortgage. They gave away prizes for mortgage applicants and had all sorts of other fluffy perks to offer. They successfully created the appearance of a very friendly environment to attract clients. However, at the "back end" of the mortgage – early renewal, prepayment privileges, etc. – they were absolutely impossible to deal with. Their clients found this out the hard way.

There is a general rule of thumb that says that the closer you are to your mortgage renewal date, the lower your penalty will be if you decide to early renew. That's because the penalty is often based on an interest differential *for the remaining term*. The longer the remaining term, the higher the penalty. So in general terms, a drop in rates would have to be very substantial to pay off if you were still in the early stages of a five-year term. However, if you were in the final year, a drop of 1 percent in rates could be an opportunity. Of course, you could only take advantage of this opportunity if you had been watching the market.

Why would you early renew at this time? If you were, say eight months away from renewal and you could bring your rate down by 1 percent that would be an attractive option, if you believed the market had reached bottom and might increase again before your renewal were due. Someone else might have an entirely different outlook, believing that rates would continue to fall right up until their renewal. They might want to stay the course and avoid the penalty, however small by this time, and take the *gamble* that rates would remain on a downward trend. I say gamble because any rate other than today's rate *is* a gamble and nobody *really* knows with any certainty where rates will go. If you don't want to gamble, you buy an insurance policy in the form of an early renewal. In this case, the penalty or blended rate is the insurance premium you pay in exchange for rate protection over the longer term.

So, it's whatever suits you. The important thing is that you make sure you have the option in your mortgage to early renew. Even over a term as short as five years, things change. Markets change. Needs change. Mortgage products change. The best possible situation is to have a mortgage with enough flexibility to change right along with you, because if it doesn't, it can inflict a great deal of financial damage. Remember all those people who were turned away by the trust company who refused to early renew? They were absolutely locked in to the 11 percent rates until renewal. What impact did that have on the original deal they negotiated? Suddenly, that extra 25 basis points off they received at the original signup wasn't looking so good anymore. As important as this particular flexibility issue is, it is seldom considered by mortgage shoppers. I would say only the top 5 percent of mortgage shoppers look out for this one. They know that the "on ramp" to a mortgage can be a challenge, but the "off ramp" can be a killer!

Your Mortgage Renewal

Some of the most notorious rate-shopping consumers, people who would do almost anything for 12.5 basis points when they are negotiating the original mortgage, go right to sleep from that point on. They do nothing even closely resembling mortgage management along the way and they certainly do little if anything to reduce costs at the time of mortgage renewal. As a result, they often rely on the original negotiation to carry them through, when in fact it only represents less than 25 percent of the job that needs to be done.

Renewal time is an opportunity to make further substantial reductions in the cost of borrowing and to pay your mortgage off years sooner. There is an abundance of opportunities at renewal time. In the current mortgage market, consumers can transfer their mortgages from institution to institution, usually without incurring additional costs. Except for the discharge fee to the outgoing financial institution (usually $75 to $150), most lenders will pay everything, including appraisals and legal fees, just to win business. This allows flexibility of choice for most people to go out and find the best deal once again.

Mortgage management done the right way is an ongoing process, beginning with the original negotiation and ending when the balance is fully repaid. The degree to which a borrower may slouch in between is the same degree to which the amortization and indeed the costs of borrowing will be increased over the life of the mortgage. People who take a proactive approach to mortgage management at all times, including renewal, end up mortgage free years sooner than those who just let it slide. I can tell you that from experience.

The following is a brief synopsis of how the average consumer handles a renewal:

• **Goes through a time of concern about interest rates usually three to six months before a renewal. They wonder where rates will be when their renewal is finally due, and in some cases lose sleep over it if market conditions are volatile.**
• **Worries about the prospect of an increased mortgage payment, knowing he or she has needlessly incurred debt, which is now straining the family budget.**
Waits for the renewal agreement to arrive, which is usually fifteen to thirty days from the renewal date itself.
• **Receives the renewal agreement, chooses a rate and term from the choices given (usually the lowest possible payment), and signs and returns the agreement to the lender along with a cheque for $85 for the renewal fee.**

You must know this example is entirely the wrong way to handle your mortgage renewal!

At renewal time, it's not just your mortgage that needs attention and review, but your entire financial plan. Remember when I said that a properly structured mortgage is the centrepiece of any wealth-creation strategy? That's still the case. At renewal, the structure of your mortgage must be reviewed to determine if it's still in line with your goals. There is no better way to decide on where you need to go than to review where you have been. Has it been three years? Perhaps five years? That's a pretty fair chunk of time. If your financial ship has been off course even a few degrees along the way you may find yourself miles away from your intended destination.

You already know the value of obtaining a copy of your credit report each year. Wouldn't it be a great help to have those reports in a file for your easy review? Wouldn't a review of your consumer borrowing habits, as documented in by your credit reports, really help you in examining the progress you have made over the last few years? Have your debts been reduced or eliminated? Good job! Have they increased? Attention is needed. Are consumer debt payments now impairing your ability to save and to weather the effects of a possible increase in mortgage payments? More attention is needed.

The rates shown on the renewal agreement you receive from your lender are really just a starting point for negotiation. The rates shown are the posted rates at the time your renewal letter was issued and are generally guaranteed for only thirty days, enough time for processing, and that's all. These rates may have fluctuated up or down, depending on market conditions, just before your renewal was issued.

At the time you receive your renewal, it may already be too late to switch your mortgage to another institution. That's because it usually takes two weeks, and sometimes longer, to transfer a mortgage. You may have to cave in to the rate being offered and that is the intended result, as lenders seek to fulfil their central mandate of maximizing profit. Lenders are very aware of this timing situation. You can short-circuit this strategy if you handle your mortgage renewal the right way.

So what's the right way? I thought it would be best to give you a recommended chronological order of events for mortgage renewal. In this fashion, you can see how it will play out. I'll explain the various steps along the way.

Ninety Days from Mortgage Renewal

This is the time when your mortgage shopping process should begin. Why? Because it is possible to acquire pre-approval from lenders with a ninety-day rate guarantee. Should there be an upswing in rates during this period, an upswing that will affect the renewal rates being offered by your existing lender, you can escape any rate escalation by exercising the ninety-day guarantee and switching your mortgage. Remember, your existing lender may only guarantee rates for the thirty-day period preceding your renewal. We know that rates can be extremely volatile at times, even over the course of a few weeks, let alone three months. So it makes sense to secure a rate early from a competing lender as an insurance policy against rate escalation.

To ignore this ninety-day window is to consciously decide to ignore all the opportunities that await you in the mortgage market, opportunities that could bring you years closer to mortgage freedom.

Begin the Shopping Process.

At this point it is necessary to haul out all of the mortgage shopping tools you gathered in chapter ten, and go to work on the mortgage market. Cast aside any loyalty you may have built up to the financial institution over the course of this term. It will only impair your judgement.

You are now into yet another sales initiative to sell your product to the highest bidder. The rules are the same as they were when you originally set up the mortgage. Watch for gimmicks. Prepare well. Know what you can afford. Repeat the whole process right through to the issuance of a pre-approval certificate with as few outstanding conditions as possible. The goal should be to win the best possible mortgage at the lowest possible cost, with a view towards reducing amortization once again, if possible. You want to exit this renewal process many steps closer to mortgage freedom.

Begin With Your Existing Lender Ninety Days Before Renewal Date.

Just as you did before, begin your shopping extravaganza with the place where you are known, your existing lender. When you get into rate discussion, you may have to pose your question twice because lenders don't always hear well the first time.

What's your rate for a five-year term? you ask.

The answer may be, Well, I can quote you today's rate but your rate will be determined thirty days from renewal. We won't know the exact rate until then.

Obviously the lender did not *really* hear you. You'll have to speak up and clearly pose your question: "I'm shopping the mortgage market to find the best possible deal for my upcoming renewal and I thought I would start here since you already have my mortgage. I'm interested in the five-year term. What's your best deal going to be?"

The lender will likely stop spouting official policy and open up the book of unofficial policy. That is, right after he gets his heart started again. Most clients, blinded by loyalty, do not approach lenders so directly. Even if they intend to shop around, they won't say so, treating it as some sort of secret. It's to your benefit to let the lender know right off the hopper that they are going to have to compete for your business all over again. The lender will realize you are immune to the judgement-impairing effects of loyalty and are a serious negotiator. They will become serious too, to your benefit. Isn't this fun? Don't forget to be carrying the latest copy of your local real-estate news opened to the page where all the lenders and brokers advertise their rates. A little quiet intimidation never hurts.

Now that the playing field has been levelled out and the power neutralized, it's time to make your best deal. So do it! If you can get a ninety-day rate guarantee, grab it and run to the next appointment. If you can't, grab the best offer you can, knowing you will likely be switching your mortgage to a new lender.

Be careful not to cave in to a final decision right then and there without shopping the market. The deal you are offered today will be just as good tomorrow and refusing to finalize will leave the door open for discovery of the treasures that await you.

Shop at Least Three Competing Lenders

Shop the market knowing there are lenders who will roll out the red carpet for you. There's nothing to fear. Remember, they want your business – they are not doing you a favour by talking to you. You are doing them a favour by giving them a shot at your business. This type of attitude opens up the doors to possibilities beyond your imagination.

Gather at least three pre-approval certificates, if you can, with ninety-day rate guarantees. Not all lenders will guarantee for ninety days – some will only go sixty. Remember, these mortgage offers are your insurance policies against rate escalation.

Sixty Days from Renewal

If you are short of mortgage offers with ninety-day guarantees, take the next best and acquire one or more sixty-day offers until you have a total of at least three competing offers other than your existing lender. A sixty-day rate guarantee is better than thirty days and it could make the difference for you.

During The Ninety-Day Waiting Period

It's a good idea to use this period to reflect on your progress and update your financial plan. You should already have determined affordability for the next term, based on your budget, with a view toward reducing amortization as much as possible, within reason. You should also look at the structure of your personal debt, if you have any, at this time. It's possible your personal debt may be getting in the way of things you'd like to do with your mortgage. There are strategies for dealing with that. I'll share an example with you later in this chapter.

Also, during this period, you should watch the mortgage market for downward fluctuations in rate. You're already protected from rates rising, so it may make sense to go out and acquire a fresh pre-approval for a newly reduced rate. They will claim to reduce your rate automatically if rates go down, but often the client will receive only a partial benefit. That's why it may make sense to secure a new offer at the lower rate.

Thirty Days from Renewal

If you were not successful in opening up the cookie jar with your existing lender, you should receive your mortgage renewal offer within this time period. If you have done your job of shopping effectively, this renewal offer should now be a worthless piece of paper. You should have successfully secured a deal much better than this and you can be confident knowing that you have protected yourself and your family to the best of your ability against unnecessary interest charges.

Make Your Decision

Your final decision should be made and an action plan executed at least three weeks before your renewal date in order to allow the transfer process to take place, if that is what you've opted for. No matter what, do not leave your decision to the last minute, as it may whittle down your options and end up increasing (or failing to decrease) the cost of borrowing.

I once heard that the biggest competitor for any business is ignorance of the market. In other words, if you are in business, your most significant competitive factor is that the market doesn't know you exist and what value your business brings. It costs a bundle to advertise and even with that, you don't have a hope of reaching everyone, so ignorance of the market will always be a factor to some degree.

The mortgage renewal process can be looked at in much the same way. You are in business to sell your product (*you*) to the mortgage market. How successful can you hope to be if you only reach one person, your existing lender? Will the lenders you don't reach magically show up on your doorstep carrying mortgage offers? I would tend to doubt it. So it seems reasonable to conclude that the more lenders you reach, the greater is the likelihood your business will be successful.

I mentioned you should reach at least three competing lenders. That's a minimum. I tempered it out of concern about the number of inquiries on the credit report having an undesirable effect on your credit score. But if you can find a way of neutralizing that effect by convincing your lenders to temporarily accept *your* copy of the credit report until you have accepted their offer, then the sky is the limit.

If you don't have to be concerned about credit score risk, is there any lender in town who should not know that your business, along with the excellent quality product that is you, is up for grabs? I don't believe so. Let the market bid for your business. You've worked hard on creating your product and you are worth more than you might at first realize. What could be better for your self-esteem and the size of your purse than a bidding war culminating in the sweetheart deal of the century? Go for it!

One more note. At renewal, you are structuring a brand new mortgage for the remaining amortization period you select. You don't automatically have to go with the same amortization you officially have remaining. That's one of the benefits of renewal – things are completely open to your best discretion. So, you can choose to reduce amortization and lessen interest charges accordingly. In most cases, you can't increase amortization without refinancing and I hope you won't need to do that anyway.

Renewal time presents an excellent opportunity to review your financial plan and get your ship back on course. It's possible to restructure your consumer debt in such a way as to complement the ultimate goal of mortgage freedom years sooner and to lay out a sensible plan for total debt elimination.

How? Well, there are a thousand possible ways, maybe more. Everyone has their own specific needs, and their financial profile is as unique as their fingerprints. So, I'm going to share with you one scenario, as an example, to demonstrate the possibilities for someone with a propensity toward debt accumulation at renewal time.

The Story of Raymond and Deborah

Raymond and Deborah Perinosky had a mortgage renewal coming due. They were concerned about recent fluctuations in interest rates, not wanting to end up with a high rate when the day came to renew. They had incurred some debt in the first five years of their mortgage. Now, with the prospect of increased mortgage payments, their debt was going to pose a bit of a problem, was going to put a squeeze on the family budget.

Raymond and Deborah, who had been virtually debt-free when they had purchased their new home, had now racked up credit card debt of $4,500. Curiously, this debt accumulation occurred after they had purchased a new vehicle which came with a hefty monthly payment of $506. The car payment had created a deficit in their family budget, a deficit of which they were not really aware. Consequently, their credit card debts began to grow as they tried to maintain the lifestyle to which they had become accustomed. The resulting increase in payments required to service the debt made the problem even worse. Little did Raymond and Deborah realize that they had already become locked into a self-perpetuating pattern of debt accumulation, bound to threaten their financial future and indeed, their newly acquired home.

The couple, fearing interest rate risk, set out early to find the best deal on their mortgage renewal, ninety days before it was due. They began by approaching their current lender, the bank where they had been doing their business for many years. They were told that renewals were only rate guaranteed in the last thirty days, and that they would do well to come back then. With the fluctuations in the market rates, the banker was not willing to commit to a rate at that time. This was not good news for Raymond and Deborah and they left the bank in despair, wondering what their loyalty to this institution had done for them over the years.

"Let's go for coffee and talk this through," said Raymond.

They ventured into the coffee shop and, for thirty minutes, argued as quietly as possible over what to do. Ride it out? Sell the house? Sell the car and take a loss? The choices were not very palatable.

Just then, Deborah squinted so she could look across the street and read a sign in the window of ABC Bank.

"Let's go."

"Where?" Raymond inquired.

"Across the street. Look at the sign."

They proceeded across the street to check things out. A sign in the window, advertising mortgage transfers with legal and appraisal fees fully paid for by the lender, had attracted Deborah's attention. "Switch your mortgage for free!"

The couple entered the bank and approached the receptionist to make an appointment.

"We saw your sign about mortgage transfers and we would like to make an appointment to see someone about that," said Deborah.

"Fine, just let me check to see what times are available."

Opening the appointment book, the receptionist found a cancellation.

"Gloria can see you right now if you like. There's been a cancellation."

Gloria was the branch mortgage lender. She had been employed by ABC for eighteen years. Fully qualified to be a branch manager, Gloria had chosen to remain in her present position. She loved interacting with clients and enjoyed the thrill of helping them design their financial future by guiding them through the first step to homeownership.

During her eighteen years, twelve managers of her branch had come and gone. Some were transferred, a few were fired and a few more quit. Gloria wanted none of that. Her work, as she had chosen it, was very rewarding for her.

This news of an immediate opportunity to see Gloria took Raymond and Deborah by surprise. They looked at each other with worry. They were intimidated by the idea of seeing a new banker. After all, they had been banking at XYZ Bank since high school and had gotten to know everyone in the branch. Now, with their financial situation under strain, the idea of switching was one they were reluctantly exploring out of necessity. They had hoped to have a couple of days to prepare, so the announcement of an immediate opening caused a bit of a flutter.

"Okay," said Raymond, while looking into Deborah's eyes for her agreement.

The receptionist led them down a long corridor to Gloria's office.

"Hi, I'm Gloria Sanderson!" Gloria introduced herself with a bright, cheerful smile, extending her hand to greet the couple. She was dressed in conservative business attire, and had the appearance of a true professional. Gloria's positive and friendly greeting had already done much to reduce Raymond and Deborah's trepidation at approaching a new banker for the first time. Perhaps this wasn't going to be such a bad experience after all.

"Hi, we're Raymond and Deborah Perrinosky."

"Very pleased to meet you! Please have a seat and make your-selves comfortable. Would you like a coffee?"

"No, thank you," said Raymond. "We just came from the coffee shop so we're just fine for now."

"Okay, then. How can I help you today?"

"We saw your sign about mortgage transfers." Deborah replied. "Ours is up for renewal on the first of June and we wanted to see what would be involved in having it transferred, that is if you can give us a good rate." Deborah's voice was still a bit shaky.

"I see. That's great! You're starting out early. It's just the first of March today." Gloria seemed quite pleased that such a young cou-ple would know the benefits of shopping the market early.

"Yes, my dad actually told me about that," Raymond replied. "He says you can sometimes get a better deal by shopping around. He told us to do it now because rates might be going up and we want to have everything arranged at today's rate."

"Your dad is certainly very wise, Raymond. Is he in banking?"

"No, he's in construction. But he read a book. I think it was called *The Friendly Banker.*"

"*The Friendly Banker*?" Gloria repeated laughing. Raymond and Gloria laughed along with her.

"Some people would say that's a contradiction in terms. I haven't read this book but your dad sure received some good advice. I do know some friendly bankers and some not so friendly as well."

"We know," said Deborah. "We just came from a meeting with one of the unfriendly kind."

"I'm sorry to hear that. Is that the bank you've been dealing with?"

"Yes it is, and we may not be there for long. They won't give us a commitment on a rate until the first of May and by that time we could be facing a rate increase," Raymond replied.

"Well, let's see what we can do for you."

Raymond and Deborah were now much more relaxed. They never dreamed a banker could be so... human! Laughing at the title *The Friendly Banker* and acknowledging that not all bankers are friendly, Gloria had exposed her own friendly side, which the couple found very reassuring and very appealing.

They proceeded through the interview stage of the mortgage application. The following is a snapshot of Raymond and Deborah's financial status, beginning with the time of their first home purchase:

Raymond & Deborah

Original Purchase Price of Home	$125,000.00
Down Payment	$6,250.00
Default Insurance Premium	$2,969.00
Total Mortgage	$121,719.00
Rate	6.95%
Term	5 years
Amortization	25 years
Monthly Payments	$848.78
Taxes & Heat	$250.00
Total Payment	$1, 098.78
Total Family Income	$4,500.00
Affordability Test # 1 (GDS Max 32%)	24.40%
Monthly Debt Payments	$50.00
Total Payments	$1,148.78
Affordability Test # two (TDS Max 40%)	25.51%
Vehicle Year: 1989	
Balance on Renewal June 1	$110,748.49

Raymond and Deborah had obtained most of the down payment for their home as a gift from their parents. They were only able to cover the legal fees themselves. Even so, they had very little debt to start out with – a $1,000 credit card balance – and their affordability ratios were well in line.

At first, they had been able to do some saving. However, the down payment on their car had wiped out everything they had saved, and the $506 a month payment on the $13,000 loan balance had increased their total debt ratio signifigantly. By the time their mortgage renewal was due, they were struggling through the twelfth month of their thirty-month car loan and debt on their credit cards had ballooned to $4,500, placing a further strain on their budget. Here was their current financial picture:

Raymond & Deborah

Balance on Renewal June 1	$110,748.49
Total Family Income	$4,700.00
Current Mortgage Payment, Taxes & Heat	$1,098.00
GDS (Max 32%)	23.36%
Credit Card Balances	$4,500.00
Car Loan Balance	$8,250.00
Total Debt Payments	
($506 + $225)	$731.00
Total Payments	$1,829.00
TDS (Max 40%)	38.91%
VehicleYear:1997	

Raymond and Deborah's income had increased slightly in three years, however, their consumer debt burden had grown from $50 per month to over $700 per month. They were now choking on debt and were facing a mortgage-rate increase they could not afford.

Gloria had finished taking their mortgage application and was looking it over, showing some concern.

"Your debt ratio is very high right now. Are you having trouble making your payments?"

"Well, we're up to date with everything, but it sometimes feels like a struggle," said Deborah.

"I can see where it would be. Perhaps we should look at a way to restructure your debt and reduce your payments at the same time as we are transferring your mortgage. That would take some of the pressure off, wouldn't it?"

"Absolutely! That would be great," replied Raymond. "How much can you reduce our payments?"

"Let me do some quick calculating and see just exactly what can be done. I'll need a few minutes. Want to do some reading while you're waiting?"

Gloria handed the couple a few brochures to read on the benefits of ABC's mortgage and investment products while she sketched out a restructuring of their debt in concert with their mortgage. Here is Gloria's proposal:

Raymond & Deborah

Balance on Renewal June 1	$110,748.49
Remaining Amortization	20 years
New Term	10 years
New Rate	6.75%
New Mortgage Payment	$440.55
	bi-weekly
New Scheduled Amortization	18 years
Actual Amortization	
(with Accelerated Bi-Weekly Payments)	15.5 years
Monthly Payment, Taxes & Heat	$1,130.00
GDS	24.04%
New Loan To Consolidate Car Loan & Cards	$12,750
Term of Loan	5 years
Monthly Payments (9% APR)	$263.65
New Total Payments	$1,397.65
New TDS	29.64%
Monthly Payment Reduction From Consolidation	$436.00
Current Mortgage Payment Increased by	$33.00
Monthly Savings Plan	$200.00
Net Payment Reduction	$200.00
New TDS with Savings Component	33.89%

A few minutes later, Raymond looked up from his pamphlets to find Gloria sitting there with a smile from ear to ear. She was positively beaming! Raymond nudged Deborah to get her attention. He wasn't sure if a smiling banker was a good sign, but somehow with Gloria he wasn't threatened by it.

"I think I may have something for you," announced Gloria. "If your mortgage could be renewed at a lower rate than you have now and your total debt payments could be reduced by $200 per month, how would that sound to you?"

"That would be great," said Deborah. "But how can you possibly do that?"

"First, I want your assurance you can afford a payment reduction of $200 and not have to use your credit cards. That's key."

"Well, I think we can," said Raymond. "We figured out our budget before we started looking into this and besides, I'm getting a long awaited raise next month that should give us another $150. It shouldn't be a problem."

"Good. In that case let me show you what I've done."

Gloria went on to explain the plan in detail. Here is a point form synopsis:

- **Gloria began by going for an immediate payment reduction by consolidating of the car loan and credit cards over a five-year term. This produced a monthly reduction of $436. The loan made sense because it was fully secured by the car, still worth $13,000. Fortunately, Raymond had set up the payments initially on a short term so his loan balance was lower as a result.**
- **Gloria decided to break up the payment reduction and use it in different ways that would benefit Raymond and Deborah. First, she budgeted for an overall payment reduction of $200. Then she allocated another $200 per month to savings. Finally, she increased the mortgage payment the couple had already been paying by $33 per month.**
- **The posted rate at the time for a five-year term was 6.95 percent. But with a discount from 7.6 percent, a 10-year term could be had for 6.75 percent. The 10-year term would protect Raymond and Deborah from further rate escalations over the next several years.**
- **By using part of the saving to increase the existing mortgage payment and then reducing the overall mortgage rate, Gloria was able to significantly reduce the total amortization from the scheduled 22 years to 18 years. Then, by applying accelerated bi-weekly payments, the amortization was further reduced to just over 15 years.**

Raymond and Deborah stared at the plan in disbelief. "You mean we will actually be into saving again?" Deborah asked.

"You will indeed. I'll introduce you later on to our financial advisor who can show you ways to invest sensibly."

"Mutual funds!" exclaimed Raymond.

"Well, not yet. Mutual funds are for long-term investments. I recommend you build up some savings first so you don't have to dip into your credit cards for emergencies. Once you have accumulated a reasonable amount you're comfortable with, then we can put you into some of the more risky, higher yield investments."

"It should be easier to save now. But what if something comes up?" asked Deborah.

"I'm going to make it even easier for you. Deborah, you and Raymond have what we call a slight propensity to overspend and incur debt. That's not to be taken as an insult. Many people, in fact most people, live paycheque to paycheque these days. Therefore, if you have this tendency it only makes common sense to use some disciplinary measures to overcome that. And better we do it now when you still have many income earning years ahead of you."

"That does make sense," said Deborah. "But what disciplinary measures?"

"I propose we debit your account every month for $200 just after your pay goes in. We'll allocate the funds to various investments that you arrange with Aaron, our financial planner. That way the money comes out right away and you'll learn to live on the rest."

"And we can afford that?" Deborah was looking for confirmation.

"You've told me an overall payment reduction of $200 was affordable, especially with Raymond's pending salary increase. This savings payment is before that has been taken into account. Also, I've calculated the payment you will be making to yourself into your debt servicing and it's still less than 34 percent, compared to almost 40 percent under your present debt structure."

"I'm a creditor?" asked Deborah.

"You certainly are and that's a very good analogy, Deborah. You should always look at yourself as a creditor. You owe a debt to yourself. That debt is the total dollar value of the amount required to shape a comfortable lifestyle in retirement for you and Raymond. It's a big debt and if you always look at yourself as the primary creditor, the one of highest importance, it will be easy to make those payments. Before you know it, the debt will be paid off and you can begin to enjoy the fruits of your labour and the benefits of your discipline."

Raymond and Deborah were excited about their newfound prospects for a better lifestyle. They certainly weren't going to be house poor – their budget was going to be generous enough, and with savings accumulating there would be no further need for credit card use. With all this in mind they were beginning to realize how their current path was leading them down a road to nowhere.

"What about the car loan?" asked Raymond. "Five years?"

"Yes. You are planning to keep it that long, aren't you?"

"I think so. In fact, I was beginning to regret getting rid of the old one. It still had miles to go and look at the trouble buying the new one caused. I think this car will last ten years!"

"Good thinking, Raymond."

"But what about the interest? Isn't it going to cost more to extend the loan to five years?" Raymond asked.

"Yes, indeed. But the benefit of the payment reduction and how we are using it, for savings, for mortgage interest reduction and for budgetary improvement, the bit of additional interest you pay on the car loan is a pittance by comparison. In addition, don't forget we are rolling in $4,500 worth of credit card debt, bringing that rate down from 18 percent to 9 percent as well."

Raymond and Debbie looked at each other and smiled.

"Can you explain what you did with the mortgage?" inquired Deborah.

"Sure. I gave you a rate discount of 85 basis points from our posted rate of 7.6 percent for a 6.75 percent 10-year rate. Then I applied $33 of your monthly savings to increase the mortgage payment you now have from $848 to $881. The slightly higher payment combined with the reduced rate and accelerated bi-weekly payments to match your bi-weekly pay periods, had the overall effect of reducing your amortization from 22 years to almost 15."

"Debbie, I think we are thousands less in debt than we were when we came here," said Raymond.

"You are, Raymond. And that's another good observation. When you look at debt, it's always best to consider the total amount in dollars that you will have to repay, not just the present balance or the rate of interest. The rate by itself can be very deceiving in its effect on your cost of borrowing. It's mainly the time factor or amortization that really affects the outcome."

"I think my dad read that in..."

"*The Friendly Banker*?" They all broke into laughter again.

"So how much did we save in real money on the mortgage?" Deborah asked.

"Well, your remaining amortization was 22 years and now it's 15, a 7-year reduction. Assuming that payment amount is not affected too much by your next renewal and we can call it an average payment for the remainder of the mortgage, $848 x 22 Years x

12 months is $223,872. That's the amount you would have had to repay."

Deborah almost fainted. "I never looked at it like that before. So how much will we pay now?"

"We'll take your current payment of $88 x 15 x 12 = $158,580. Subtracted from $223,872, I would say you are going to miss out on over $64,000 in mortgage payments."

"The $64,000 question," Raymond quipped.

"No, the $64,000 *answer*," replied Deborah.

"You've got it!" They all laughed once again.

Gloria continued. "I thought it was best that given your slight propensity towards overspending, which I know you're going to control, that we build an insurance policy for you just in case. The insurance policy is the fast track to mortgage freedom. You're both twenty-eight now. You will be mortgage free by forty-three instead of fifty."

"Mortgage free by forty-three," replied Raymond. "I like the sound of that. It rhymes." Deborah gave him a nudge.

"I sure don't want to be making mortgage payments when I'm fifty," Deborah replied.

Gloria went on to say, "Just imagine, you two, you're going to begin saving now. But what if at forty-three, once your mortgage is paid off, you continue to make the mortgage payments, only to yourselves?"

"The possibilities are endless!" replied Raymond.

"By the way, what are the possibilities exactly?" Deborah rolled her eyes.

"Well, taking your average mortgage payment of $881, if you decided to retire at sixty-five and paid yourself that amount from age forty-three, assuming a return of only 8 percent compounded annually to be conservative, you would have over $600,000 plus any accumulated tax savings from RRSP investments. That's in addition to whatever you have saved along the way."

"We've won the lottery," said Raymond.

"Well, not yet. But you're on the right track. By the way, your consolidation loan will be paid off in five years. You will then be able to add that additional payment amount, $263.65, to the retirement debt you owe yourself for the following five years until you are ready for another vehicle. That will give you another $20,000 or so."

"The saving just never ends!" exclaimed Raymond.

"I'm happy you're happy," Gloria added. "But one cautionary note: what we have been talking about here is a financial plan for your retirement. It's a good start but it's not the whole picture. I recommend you continually use the services of an experienced and professional financial planner on an ongoing basis."

"Why's that?" asked Deborah. "This plan seems incredible!"

"Like I said, it's a good start. Certainly, it's monumentally better than the plan you came in here with, with all due respect to you both. However, any plan you make today, no matter how good, no matter how many contingencies it may cover, there will always be bumps in the road. There will always be times when your discipline will be challenged, when debt will try and move in again to upset your plan, when the completely unexpected event happens. It's at these times that we run the risk of going off course. So we need someone with an unbiased view to help us adjust and make sure we stay on track towards paying off the retirement debt we owe ourselves. The financial plan you have today may be unrecognizable to you in five years. Things just change so fast."

"They sure do," added Raymond. "Let me get this straight. About an hour ago, we came in here without an appointment, concerned about rates going up and in debt, with what looked like no solution and certainly no financial plan for retirement. We thought we may have to sell our car or our house or both. In the space of sixty minutes, we have a lower rate on our mortgage, thousands of savings, a consolidated loan by which we save even more and the beginnings of a solid plan for our future retirement. Do I have my facts straight?"

"Yes you do." Gloria smiled humbly.

"Gloria, I think Debbie and I have made a decision to take your offer, haven't we hon?"

"We sure have. Can we get this in motion right away, Gloria?"

"I'll prepare the paperwork for your signature tomorrow when you can also have your session with Aaron."

With that, Raymond and Deborah departed Gloria's company for this day, looking back to catch another glimpse of her smiling face as she waved from the doorway of her office. When they were safely outside they breathed a sigh of relief and hugged one another. Their financial future had been set back on course. Their financial worries had all but disappeared. They could remain in their home. For the first time they understood the value of planning for the future. They had also experienced first-hand the feeling of desperation caused by the lack of financial discipline, and had glimpsed some of the consequences. They vowed this situation would never repeat itself, and it never did. Raymond and Deborah had, at last, met a friendly banker.

This story demonstrates many things. Among the most important is the role debt can play in derailing your plans for a comfortable retirement. We're not necessarily talking about lavish riches here. Realistically we know that most people will never reach that plateau. But comfort is certainly worth striving for. If riches come after that, so much the better. This story also teaches the lesson that a properly structured mortgage really is the centrepiece of your wealth-creation strategy. When you set up a mortgage, it must be structured in such a way as to meet the requirements of your financial plan. Any lesser approach is bound to steer you miles off course, and as we have seen, run the risk of grounding your financial ship on the rocks of a deserted beach.

We can see, by the snapshot of Raymond and Deborah's original mortgage transaction, that they had had the ability to take a reduced amortization when they first bought the house. But they had given up that opportunity in exchange for the lowest possible payment, as most consumers do. The reduced payment is a comfort zone based in fantasyland. It creates a false sense of financial well being that causes some people, thinking everything is wonderful, to be comfortable incurring even more debt. This is one of the tragic consequences of "The E Factor."

Rest assured, the accumulation of all of the financial decisions you have made to date has brought you to the place you're at right now. It does concern me a great deal, as you can probably tell, when I see people making these reckless decisions almost every day, for I have seen the effects of the accumulation of bad decisions influenced by "The E Factor". It's that tendency to delay, to put it off, to take what seems to be the easiest route that builds a mountain of regret in later years just at a time when the vitality and the financial resources needed to cure it all seem fleeting.

For those with a more aggressive "E Factor" those who may have a tendency toward debt accumulation, the price paid can be much higher. Consumer debt can interfere so greatly with the desire for mortgage freedom that it protracts the amortization of a mortgage into outer space. Too often, the occupant of the space ship cannot live long enough to enjoy the fruits of a lifetime of labour.

That's the bad news. The good news is if you realize the direction your actions are taking you early enough, you can reverse the course and bring mortgage freedom, together with a comfortable retirement, back into focus. What a glorious result that could be for you. The key is to recognize it, to bite the bullet of discipline and to set a new financial plan in motion without delay.

I sincerely hope you feel that you now have all of the tools necessary to make a measurable difference in your life. All it takes now is action. Start today and you will begin to fashion a more comfortable lifestyle for yourself both now and in retirement, with all of the joy and peace of mind that can bring. I wish that for you. May God bless.

And thank you, Mr. Whitby, wherever you are.

Index